indian

100 everyday recipes

First published in 2011
LOVE FOOD is an imprint of Parragon Books Ltd

Parragon
Chartist House
15-17 Trim Street
Bath BA1 1HA, UK
www.parragon.com

ISBN: 978-1-4454-3042-3

Printed in China

Produced by Ivy Contract
Photography by Charlie Paul

Notes for the Reader

This book uses both metric and imperial measurements. Follow the same units of measurement throughout; do not mix metric and imperial. All spoon measurements are level: teaspoons are assumed to be 5 ml, and tablespoons are assumed to be 15 ml. Unless otherwise stated, milk is assumed to be full fat, eggs and individual vegetables are medium, and pepper is freshly ground black pepper.

The times given are an approximate guide only. Preparation times differ according to the techniques used by different people and the cooking times may also vary from those given. Optional ingredients, variations or serving suggestions have not been included in the calculations.

Recipes using raw or very lightly cooked eggs should be avoided by infants, the elderly, pregnant women, convalescents and anyone suffering from an illness. Pregnant and breastfeeding women are advised to avoid eating peanuts and peanut products. Sufferers from nut allergies should be aware that some of the ready-made ingredients used in the recipes in this book may contain nuts. Always check the packaging before use. Vegetarians should be aware that some of the ready-made ingredients used in the recipes in this book may contain animal products. Always check the packaging before use.

indian

introduction

Nowadays, supermarkets stock ingredients from across the world and city streets are lined with restaurants representing every imaginable country. In the West, Indian cooking is among the most popular of eastern cuisines, especially now that keen home cooks have discovered how easy it is to prepare authentic, tasty and nutritious Indian dishes. Perhaps the secrets of its popularity are its subtlety and extraordinary variety.

Given that the sub-continent is so huge, with an equally extensive history, it is hardly surprising that both its people and their diets are so diverse. Religious practices have had a profound influence — Hindus don't eat beef, Muslims don't eat pork and Buddhists, among others, are vegetarian. Explorers, conquerors and colonizers have had an effect too, clearly seen in the rich-tasting dishes created for Moghul emperors or the use of vinegar in the curries of former Portuguese territories, for example. Foreign ingredients are most often seen in the dishes of western India. Climate and topography also play their part and each region of the country has a unique style of cooking based on local ingredients. In the north, dairy

products such as yogurt and ghee (clarified butter) are featured, as well as nuts, while southern cooking is characterized by its use of coconuts, their oil and a variety of chillies. Eastern regions are famous for their fish dishes and mustard oil. Delhi is well known for tandoori cooking, Kashmir for its meat, especially lamb, Madras for its wealth of vegetarian dishes and Bengal for fine fish and tooth-achingly sweet desserts.

However, the cuisines of all regions are united in the use of careful blends of spices, which are usually bought whole and ground as needed. These mixtures are subtle and aromatic but not invariably hot, although both fresh and dried chillies do feature in many dishes. With such a wide variety of choice, why not let Indian cuisine add a touch of spice to your culinary repertoire?

chicken

chicken dopiaza

ingredients

serves 4

700 g/1 lb 9 oz skinless, boneless
  chicken breasts or thighs
juice of ½ lemon
1 tsp salt, or to taste
5 tbsp sunflower or olive oil
2 large onions, roughly chopped
5 large garlic cloves, roughly chopped
2.5-cm/1-inch piece fresh ginger,
  roughly chopped
2 tbsp whole milk natural yogurt
2.5-cm/1-inch piece cinnamon
  stick, halved
4 green cardamom pods, bruised
4 cloves
½ tsp black peppercorns
½ tsp ground turmeric
½ –1 tsp chilli powder
1 tsp ground coriander
4 tbsp passata
150 ml/5 fl oz warm water
½ tsp granulated sugar
8 shallots, halved
1 tsp garam masala
2 tbsp chopped fresh coriander
  leaves
1 tomato, chopped
Indian bread, to serve

method

1 Cut the chicken into 2.5-cm/1-inch cubes. Add the
  lemon juice and half the salt and rub well into the
  chicken. Cover and leave to marinate for 20 minutes.

2 Heat 1 tablespoon of the oil in a small saucepan over
  a medium heat, add the onions, garlic and ginger and
  cook, stirring frequently, for 4–5 minutes. Leave to
  cool slightly. Add the yogurt and blend to a purée.

3 Heat 3 tablespoons of the remaining oil in a medium
  heavy-based saucepan over a low heat, add the
  cinnamon stick, cardamom pods, cloves and
  peppercorns and cook, stirring, for 25–30 seconds.
  Add the puréed ingredients, and cook for 5 minutes.

4 Add the turmeric, chilli powder and ground coriander
  and cook, stirring, for 2 minutes. Add the passata and
  cook, stirring, for 3 minutes. Increase the heat slightly,
  then add the marinated chicken and cook, stirring,
  until it changes colour. Add the warm water, the
  remaining salt and the sugar. Bring to the boil, then
  reduce the heat to low, cover and cook for 20 minutes.

5 Heat the remaining oil in a small saucepan, add the
  shallots and stir-fry. Add the garam masala, stir the
  shallot mixture into the curry and simmer. Add the
  fresh coriander and chopped tomato and remove from
  the heat. Serve immediately with Indian bread.

chicken korma

ingredients

serves 4

1 chicken, weighing
   1.3 kg/3 lb
225 g/8 oz ghee or butter
3 onions, thinly sliced
1 garlic clove, crushed
2.5-cm/1-inch piece fresh
   ginger, grated
1 tsp mild chilli powder
1 tsp ground turmeric
1 tsp ground coriander
½ tsp ground cardamom
½ tsp ground cinnamon
½ tsp salt
1 tbsp gram flour
125 ml/4 fl oz milk
500 ml/18 fl oz double cream
fresh coriander leaves,
   to garnish
freshly cooked rice, to serve

method

1 Put the chicken into a large saucepan, cover with water and bring to the boil. Reduce the heat, cover and simmer for 30 minutes. Remove from the heat, lift out the chicken and set aside to cool. Reserve 125 ml/4 fl oz of the cooking liquid. Remove and discard the skin and bones. Cut the flesh into bite-sized pieces.

2 Heat the ghee in a large saucepan over a medium heat. Add the onions and garlic and cook, stirring, for 3 minutes, or until softened. Add the ginger, chilli powder, turmeric, ground coriander, cardamom, cinnamon and salt and cook for a further 5 minutes. Add the chicken and the reserved cooking liquid. Cook for 2 minutes.

3 Blend the flour with a little of the milk and add to the pan, then stir in the remaining milk. Bring to the boil, stirring, then reduce the heat, cover and simmer for 25 minutes. Stir in the cream, cover and simmer for a further 15 minutes.

4 Garnish with coriander leaves and serve with freshly cooked rice.

kashmiri chicken

ingredients

serves 4–6

seeds from 8 green cardamom
    pods
¹/₂ tsp coriander seeds
¹/₂ tsp cumin seeds
1 cinnamon stick
8 black peppercorns
6 cloves
1 tbsp hot water
¹/₂ tsp saffron threads
40 g/1¹/₂ oz ghee or 3 tbsp
    vegetable or groundnut oil
1 large onion, finely chopped
2 tbsp garlic and ginger paste
250 ml/9 fl oz natural yogurt
8 skinless, boneless chicken thighs,
    sliced
3 tbsp ground almonds
55 g/2 oz blanched pistachio nuts,
    finely chopped
2 tbsp chopped fresh coriander
2 tbsp chopped fresh mint
salt
toasted flaked almonds,
    to garnish
Indian bread, to serve

method

1 Dry-roast the cardamom seeds in a frying pan over
    a medium–low heat, stirring constantly, until you can
    smell the aroma. Repeat with the coriander and cumin
    seeds, cinnamon, peppercorns and cloves. Put all the
    spices, except the cinnamon stick, in a spice grinder
    and grind to a powder.

2 Put the hot water and saffron threads in a small bowl
    and set aside. Melt the ghee in a flameproof casserole.
    Add the onion and cook, stirring occasionally, over
    a medium–high heat for 5–8 minutes. Add the garlic
    and ginger paste and continue stirring for 2 minutes.

3 Stir in the ground spices and the cinnamon stick.
    Remove from the heat and mix in the yogurt, a small
    amount at a time, stirring vigorously, then return to
    the heat and continue stirring for 2–3 minutes, until
    the ghee separates. Add the chicken pieces.

4 Bring to the boil, stirring constantly, then reduce the
    heat to low, cover and simmer for 20 minutes, stirring
    occasionally. Stir in the ground almonds, pistachios,
    saffron with its soaking liquid, half the coriander, all
    the mint and salt to taste. Re-cover the pan and simmer
    for about 5 minutes, until the chicken is tender and
    the sauce is thickened. Sprinkle with coriander
    and the flaked almonds and serve with Indian bread.

balti chicken

ingredients

serves 6

3 tbsp ghee or vegetable oil

2 large onions, sliced

3 tomatoes, sliced

½ tsp kalonji seeds

4 black peppercorns

2 green cardamom pods

1 cinnamon stick

1 tsp chilli powder

1 tsp garam masala

2 tsp garlic and ginger paste

700 g/1 lb 9 oz skinless, boneless
    chicken breasts or thighs, diced

2 tbsp natural yogurt

2 tbsp chopped fresh coriander,
    plus extra sprigs to garnish

2 fresh green chillies, deseeded
    and finely chopped

2 tbsp lime juice

salt

method

1 Heat the ghee in a large heavy-based frying pan.
    Add the onions and cook over a low heat, stirring
    occasionally, for 10 minutes, or until golden. Add the
    tomatoes, kalonji seeds, peppercorns, cardamom pods,
    cinnamon stick, chilli powder, garam masala, and garlic
    and ginger paste, and season to taste with salt. Cook,
    stirring constantly, for 5 minutes.

2 Add the chicken and cook, stirring constantly, for
    5 minutes, or until well coated in the spice paste. Stir
    in the yogurt. Cover and simmer, stirring occasionally,
    for 10 minutes.

3 Stir in the chopped coriander, chillies and lime juice.
    Transfer to a warmed serving dish, garnish with
    coriander sprigs and serve immediately.

variation

Add 200 g/7 oz broccoli divided into very small florets
and 85 g/3 oz small peas to the pan, plus 50 ml/2 fl oz
chicken stock, when the chicken has finished its initial
cooking. Increase the simmering time to 12 minutes.

chicken tikka masala

ingredients

serves 4–6

400 g/14 oz canned chopped
   tomatoes
300 ml/10 fl oz double cream
8 cooked tandoori chicken pieces
   (see page 28)
salt and pepper
fresh chopped coriander,
   to garnish
cooked basmati rice, to serve

tikka masala

30 g/1 oz ghee or 2 tbsp vegetable
   or groundnut oil
1 large garlic clove, finely chopped
1 fresh red chilli, deseeded and
   chopped
2 tsp ground cumin
2 tsp ground paprika
½ tsp salt
pepper

method

1 To make the tikka masala, melt the ghee in a large
   frying pan with a lid over a medium heat. Add the
   garlic and chilli and stir-fry for 1 minute. Stir in the cumin,
   paprika and salt and pepper to taste and continue
   stirring for about 30 seconds.

2 Stir the tomatoes and cream into the tikka masala.
   Reduce the heat to low and leave the sauce to simmer
   for about 10 minutes, stirring frequently, until it reduces
   and thickens.

3 Meanwhile, remove all the bones and any skin from
   the tandoori chicken pieces, then cut the meat into
   bite-sized pieces.

4 Adjust the seasoning of the sauce, if necessary. Add
   the chicken pieces to the pan, cover and leave to
   simmer for 3–5 minutes, until the chicken is heated
   through. Garnish with coriander and serve with
   cooked basmati rice.

butter chicken

ingredients

serves 4–6

1 onion, chopped
1½ tbsp garlic and ginger paste
400 g/14 oz canned chopped
    tomatoes
¼–½ tsp chilli powder
pinch of sugar
30 g/1 oz ghee or 2 tbsp vegetable
    or groundnut oil
125 ml/4 fl oz water
1 tbsp tomato purée
40 g/1½ oz butter, cut into
    small pieces
½ tsp garam masala
½ tsp ground cumin
½ tsp ground coriander
8 cooked tandoori chicken pieces
4 tbsp double cream
salt and pepper
chopped cashew nuts and fresh
    coriander sprigs, to garnish

method

1 Put the onion and garlic and ginger paste in a food processor, blender or spice grinder and whizz together until a paste forms. Add the tomatoes, chilli powder, sugar and a pinch of salt and whizz again until blended.

2 Melt the ghee in a wok or large frying pan over a medium–high heat. Add the tomato mixture and water and stir in the tomato pureé.

3 Bring the mixture to the boil, stirring, then reduce the heat to very low and simmer for 5 minutes, stirring occasionally, until the sauce thickens.

4 Stir in half the butter, the garam masala, cumin and coriander. Add the chicken pieces and stir around until they are well coated. Simmer for a further 10 minutes, or until the chicken is hot. Taste and adjust the seasoning, if necessary.

5 Lightly beat the cream in a small bowl and stir in several tablespoons of the hot sauce, beating constantly. Stir the cream mixture into the tomato sauce, then add the remaining butter and stir until it melts. Garnish with the chopped cashew nuts and coriander sprigs and serve straight from the pan.

wok-cooked chicken in tomato & fenugreek sauce

ingredients

serves 4

700 g/1 lb 9 oz skinless, boneless
  chicken thighs, cut into
  2.5-cm/1-inch cubes
juice of 1 lime
1 tsp salt, or to taste
4 tbsp sunflower or olive oil
1 large onion, finely chopped
2 tsp ginger purée
2 tsp garlic purée
⅓ tsp ground turmeric
½–1 tsp chilli powder
1 tbsp ground coriander
425 g/15 oz canned chopped
  tomatoes
125 ml/4 fl oz warm water
1 tbsp dried fenugreek leaves
½ tsp garam masala
2 tbsp chopped fresh coriander
  leaves
2–4 fresh green chillies
Indian bread, to serve

method

1 Place the chicken in a non-metallic bowl and rub in the lime juice and salt. Cover and set aside for 30 minutes.

2 Heat the oil in a wok or heavy-based frying pan over a medium–high heat. Add the onion and stir-fry for 7–8 minutes, until it begins to colour.

3 Add the ginger and garlic purées and continue to stir-fry for about a minute. Add the turmeric, chilli powder and ground coriander, then reduce the heat slightly and cook the spices for 25–30 seconds. Add half the tomatoes, stir-fry for 3–4 minutes and add the remaining tomatoes. Continue to cook, stirring, until the tomato juice has evaporated and the oil separates from the spice paste and floats on the surface.

4 Add the chicken and increase the heat to high. Stir-fry for 4–5 minutes, then add the warm water, reduce the heat to medium–low and cook for 8–10 minutes, or until the sauce has thickened and the chicken is tender.

5 Add the fenugreek leaves, garam masala, half the coriander leaves and the chillies. Cook for 1–2 minutes, remove from the heat and transfer to a serving plate. Garnish with the remaining coriander and serve with Indian bread.

chicken with stir-fried spices

ingredients

serves 4

700 g/1 lb 9 oz skinless, boneless chicken breasts or thighs
juice of ½ lemon
1 tsp salt, or to taste
5 tbsp sunflower or olive oil
1 large onion, finely chopped
2 tsp garlic purée
2 tsp ginger purée
½ tsp ground turmeric
1 tsp ground cumin
2 tsp ground coriander
½–1 tsp chilli powder
150 g/5½ oz canned chopped tomatoes
150 ml/5 fl oz warm water
1 large garlic clove, finely chopped
1 small or ½ large red pepper, deseeded and cut into 2.5-cm/1-inch pieces
1 small or ½ large green pepper, deseeded and cut into 2.5-cm/1-inch pieces
1 tsp garam masala
Indian bread, to serve

method

1 Cut the chicken into 2.5-cm/1-inch cubes and put in a non-metallic bowl. Add the lemon juice and half the salt and rub well into the chicken. Cover and leave to marinate in the refrigerator for 20 minutes.

2 Heat 4 tablespoons of the oil in a medium heavy-based saucepan over a medium heat. Add the onion and cook, stirring frequently, for 8–9 minutes, until lightly browned. Add the garlic and ginger purées and cook, stirring, for 3 minutes. Add the turmeric, cumin, coriander and chilli powder and cook, stirring, for 1 minute. Add the tomatoes and their juice and cook for 2–3 minutes, stirring frequently, until the oil separates from the spice paste.

3 Add the marinated chicken, increase the heat slightly and cook, stirring, until it changes colour. Add the warm water and bring to the boil. Reduce the heat, cover and simmer for 25 minutes.

4 Heat the remaining 1 tablespoon of oil in a small saucepan or frying pan over a low heat. Add the garlic and cook, stirring frequently, until browned. Add the peppers, increase the heat to medium and stir-fry for 2 minutes, then stir in the garam masala. Fold the pepper mixture into the curry. Remove from the heat and serve immediately with Indian bread.

cumin-scented chicken

ingredients

serves 4

700 g/1 lb 9 oz boneless chicken thighs or breasts, cut into 5-cm/2-inch pieces
juice of 1 lime
1 tsp salt, or to taste
3 tbsp sunflower or olive oil
1 tsp cumin seeds
2.5-cm/1-inch piece cinnamon stick
5 green cardamom pods, bruised
4 cloves
1 large onion, finely chopped
2 tsp garlic purée
2 tsp ginger purée
½ tsp ground turmeric
2 tsp ground cumin
½ tsp chilli powder
225 g/8 oz canned chopped tomatoes
1 tbsp tomato purée
½ tsp sugar
225 ml/8 fl oz warm water
½ tsp garam masala
2 tbsp chopped fresh coriander leaves, plus extra sprigs to garnish
Indian bread, to serve

method

1 Put the chicken in a non-metallic bowl and rub in the lime juice and salt. Cover and set aside for 30 minutes.

2 Heat the oil in a medium saucepan over a low heat and add the cumin seeds, cinnamon, cardamom and cloves. Let them sizzle for 25–30 seconds, then add the onion. Cook, stirring regularly, for 5 minutes, or until the onion is soft.

3 Add the garlic and ginger purées and cook for about a minute, then add the turmeric, ground cumin and chilli powder. Add the tomatoes, tomato purée and sugar. Cook over a medium heat, stirring regularly, until the tomatoes reach a paste-like consistency and the oil separates from the paste. Sprinkle over a little water if the mixture sticks to the pan.

4 Add the chicken and increase the heat to medium–high. Stir until the chicken changes colour, then pour in the warm water. Bring to the boil, reduce the heat to medium–low and cook for 12–15 minutes, or until the sauce has thickened and the chicken is tender.

5 Stir in the garam masala and chopped coriander. Transfer to a serving dish and garnish with coriander sprigs. Serve with Indian bread.

chicken biryani

ingredients

serves 8

small piece fresh ginger
1½ tsp crushed garlic
1 tbsp garam masala
1 tsp chilli powder
2 tsp salt
5 green cardamom pods, bruised
300 ml/10 fl oz natural yogurt
1 chicken, weighing 1.5 kg/
    3 lb 5 oz
150 ml/5 fl oz milk
1½ tsp saffron strands
6 tbsp ghee
2 onions, sliced
450 g/1 lb basmati rice
2 cinnamon sticks
4 fresh green chillies
2 tbsp coriander leaves
4 tbsp lemon juice

method

1 Finely chop the ginger, then put it in a bowl with the garlic, garam masala, chilli powder, half the salt, and the cardamom pods. Add the yogurt. Skin the chicken, cut into 8 pieces, then add the pieces to the yoghurt mixture and mix well. Cover and leave to marinate in the refrigerator for 3 hours.

2 Pour the milk into a small saucepan, bring to the boil, then sprinkle over the saffron and reserve. Heat the ghee in a saucepan. Add the onions and fry until golden. Transfer half of the onions and ghee to a bowl and reserve.

3 Place the rice and cinnamon sticks in a saucepan of water. Bring the rice to the boil and simmer for 4–5 minutes, then remove from the heat. Drain and place in a bowl. Mix with the remaining salt.

4 Chop the chillies and coriander leaves and reserve. Add the chicken mixture to the saucepan containing the onions. Add half each of the chopped green chillies, lemon juice, coriander and saffron milk. Add the rice, then the rest of the ingredients, including the reserved onions and ghee. Cover tightly. Cook over a low heat for 1 hour. Check that the meat is cooked through; if it is not cooked, return to the heat and cook for a further 15 minutes. Mix well before serving.

tandoori chicken

ingredients

serves 4

4 chicken pieces, about
    225 g/8 oz each, skinned
juice of 1/2 lemon
1/2 tsp salt, or to taste
85 g/3 oz whole milk natural
    yogurt, strained, or
    Greek-style yogurt
3 tbsp double cream
1 tbsp gram flour
1 tbsp garlic purée
1 tbsp ginger purée
1/2–1 tsp chilli powder
1 tsp ground coriander
1/2 tsp ground cumin
1/2 tsp garam masala
1/2 tsp ground turmeric
2 tbsp vegetable oil,
    for brushing
3 tbsp melted butter or olive oil
lemon wedges, to garnish
salad, to serve

method

1 Make 2–3 small incisions in each chicken piece and place in a large non-metallic bowl. Rub in the lemon juice and salt, cover and chill in the refrigerator for 20 minutes.

2 Meanwhile, put the yogurt in a separate bowl and add the cream and gram flour. Beat with a fork until well blended and smooth. Add all the remaining ingredients, except the oil and melted butter, and mix thoroughly. Pour over the chicken and rub in well. Cover and chill in the refrigerator for 4–6 hours, or overnight. Return to room temperature before cooking.

3 Preheat the grill to high. Line a grill pan with foil and brush the rack with oil. Using tongs, lift the chicken pieces out of the marinade and put on the prepared rack, reserving the remaining marinade. Cook the chicken under the preheated grill for 4 minutes, then turn over and cook for a further 4 minutes. Baste the chicken generously with the reserved marinade and cook for a further 2 minutes on each side.

4 Brush the chicken with the melted butter and cook for 5–6 minutes. Turn over and baste with the remaining marinade. Cook for 5–6 minutes, until the juices run clear when a skewer is inserted into the meat.

5 Transfer the chicken to a dish. Serve with salad and garnish with lemon wedges.

silky chicken kebabs

ingredients

serves 8

55 g/2 oz raw cashew nuts
2 tbsp single cream
1 egg
450 g/1 lb skinless, boneless
    chicken breasts, roughly
    chopped
½ tsp salt, or to taste
2 tsp garlic purée
2 tsp ginger purée
2 fresh green chillies, roughly
    chopped (deseeded
    if you like)
15 g/½ oz fresh coriander,
    including the tender stalks,
    roughly chopped
1 tsp garam masala
vegetable oil, for brushing
25 g/1 oz butter, melted
chutney, to serve

method

1 Put the cashew nuts in a heatproof bowl, cover with boiling water and leave to soak for 20 minutes. Drain and put in a food processor. Add the cream and egg and process the ingredients to a coarse mixture.

2 Add all the remaining ingredients, except the oil and melted butter, and process until smooth. Transfer to a bowl, cover and chill in the refrigerator for 30 minutes.

3 Preheat the grill to high. Brush the rack and 8 metal or pre-soaked wooden skewers lightly with oil. Have a bowl of cold water ready.

4 Divide the chilled mixture into 8 equal-sized portions. Dip your hands into the bowl of cold water – this will stop the mixture sticking to your fingers when you are moulding it onto the skewers. Carefully mould each portion onto a skewer, forming it into a 15-cm/6-inch sausage shape. Arrange the kebabs on the prepared rack and cook under the preheated grill for 4 minutes. Brush with half the melted butter and cook for a further minute. Turn over and cook for 3 minutes. Baste with the remaining melted butter and cook for a further 2 minutes.

5 Remove from the heat and leave the kebabs to rest for 5 minutes before sliding them off the skewers with a knife. Serve with chutney.

meat

lamb rogan josh

ingredients

serves 4

350 ml/12 fl oz natural yogurt

½ tsp ground asafoetida, dissolved in 2 tbsp water

700 g/1 lb 9 oz boneless leg of lamb, trimmed and cut into 5-cm/2-inch cubes

2 tomatoes, deseeded and chopped

1 onion, chopped

25 g/1 oz ghee or 2 tbsp vegetable or groundnut oil

1½ tbsp garlic and ginger paste

2 tbsp tomato purée

2 bay leaves

1 tbsp ground coriander

¼–1 tsp chilli powder, ideally Kashmiri chilli powder

½ tsp ground turmeric

1 tsp salt

½ tsp garam masala

method

1 Put the yogurt in a large bowl and stir in the dissolved asafoetida. Add the lamb and use your hands to rub in all the marinade, then set aside for 30 minutes.

2 Meanwhile, put the tomatoes and onion in a blender and process until blended.

3 Melt the ghee in a flameproof casserole or large frying pan with a tight-fitting lid. Add the garlic and ginger paste and stir around until the aromas are released. Stir in the tomato mixture, tomato purée, bay leaves, coriander, chilli powder and turmeric, reduce the heat to low and simmer, stirring occasionally, for 5–8 minutes.

4 Add the lamb and salt with any leftover marinade and stir around for 2 minutes. Cover, reduce the heat to low and simmer, stirring occasionally, for 30 minutes. The lamb should give off enough moisture to prevent it from catching on the base of the pan, but if the sauce looks too dry, stir in a little water.

5 Sprinkle with the garam masala, re-cover the pan and continue simmering for 15–20 minutes, until the lamb is tender. Serve immediately.

lamb dopiaza

ingredients

serves 4

4 onions, sliced into rings
3 garlic cloves, roughly chopped
2.5-cm/1-inch piece fresh
    ginger, grated
1 tsp ground coriander
1 tsp ground cumin
1 tsp chilli powder
½ tsp ground turmeric
1 tsp ground cinnamon
1 tsp garam masala
4 tbsp water
5 tbsp ghee or vegetable oil
600 g/1 lb 5 oz boneless lamb,
    cut into bite-sized chunks
6 tbsp natural yogurt
salt and pepper
fresh coriander leaves,
    to garnish
cooked basmati rice, to serve

method

1 Put half of the onions into a food processor with the garlic, ginger, ground coriander, cumin, chilli powder, turmeric, cinnamon and garam masala. Add the water and process to a paste.

2 Heat 4 tablespoons of the ghee in a saucepan over a medium heat. Add the remaining onions and cook, stirring, for 3 minutes. Remove from the heat. Lift out the onions with a slotted spoon and set aside. Heat the remaining ghee in the pan over a high heat, add the lamb and cook, stirring, for 5 minutes. Lift out the meat and drain on kitchen paper.

3 Add the onion paste to the pan and cook over a medium heat, stirring, until the oil separates. Stir in the yogurt, season to taste with salt and pepper, return the lamb to the pan and stir well.

4 Bring the mixture gently to the boil, reduce the heat, cover and simmer for 25 minutes. Stir in the reserved onion rings and cook for a further 5 minutes. Remove from the heat, and garnish with coriander leaves. Serve immediately with cooked basmati rice.

lamb pasanda

ingredients

serves 4–6

600 g/1 lb 5 oz boneless shoulder
    or leg of lamb
2 tbsp garlic and ginger paste
55 g/2 oz ghee or 4 tbsp vegetable
    or groundnut oil
3 large onions, chopped
1 fresh green chilli, deseeded
    and chopped
2 green cardamom pods, bruised
1 cinnamon stick, broken
    in half
2 tsp ground coriander
1 tsp ground cumin
1 tsp ground turmeric
250 ml/9 fl oz water
150 ml/5 fl oz double cream
4 tbsp ground almonds
1½ tsp salt
1 tsp garam masala
paprika and toasted flaked
    almonds, to garnish

method

1 Cut the meat into thin slices, then place the slices
between clingfilm and pound with a meat mallet.
Put the lamb slices in a bowl, add the garlic and ginger
paste and rub well into the lamb. Cover and leave to
marinate in the refrigerator for 2 hours.

2 Melt the ghee in a large frying pan over a medium–
high heat. Add the onions and chilli and cook, stirring
frequently, for 5–8 minutes, until golden brown.

3 Stir in the cardamom pods, cinnamon stick, ground
coriander, cumin and turmeric and continue stirring
for 2 minutes, or until the spices are aromatic. Add
the meat to the pan and cook, stirring occasionally,
for about 5 minutes, until it is brown on all sides
and the fat begins to separate. Stir in the water and
bring to the boil, still stirring. Reduce the heat to its
lowest setting, cover the pan tightly and simmer for
40 minutes, or until the meat is tender.

4 Mix the cream and ground almonds together in a
bowl. Beat in 6 tablespoons of the hot cooking liquid
from the pan, then gradually beat this mixture back
into the pan. Stir in the salt and garam masala. Simmer
for a further 5 minutes, uncovered, stirring occasionally.

5 Garnish with a sprinkling of paprika and flaked
almonds and serve.

lamb, tomato & aubergine curry

ingredients

serves 4

2 tbsp oil
500 g/1 lb 2 oz lamb fillet or leg,
    cut into cubes
1 large onion, coarsely chopped
2–3 tbsp curry paste
1 aubergine, cut into small cubes
10 tomatoes, peeled, deseeded
    and coarsely chopped
400 ml/14 fl oz coconut milk
300 ml/10 fl oz lamb stock
2 tbsp chopped fresh coriander,
    plus extra sprigs to garnish

method

1 Heat the oil in a large frying pan. Add the lamb in batches and cook for 8–10 minutes, or until browned all over. Remove with a slotted spoon and reserve.

2 Add the onion to the frying pan and cook for 2–3 minutes, or until just softened. Add the curry paste and stir-fry for a further 2 minutes. Add the aubergine, three-quarters of the tomatoes and the lamb and stir together.

3 Add the coconut milk and stock and simmer gently for 30–40 minutes, until the lamb is tender and the curry has thickened.

4 Mix the remaining tomatoes and the chopped coriander together in a bowl, then stir into the curry. Garnish with coriander sprigs and serve immediately.

peshawar-style lamb curry

ingredients

serves 4

4 tbsp sunflower or olive oil
2.5-cm/1-inch piece
    cinnamon stick
5 green cardamom pods, bruised
5 cloves
2 bay leaves
700 g/1 lb 9 oz boneless leg of
    lamb, cut into 2.5-cm/
    1-inch cubes
1 large onion, finely chopped
2 tsp ginger purée
2 tsp garlic purée
1 tbsp tomato purée
1 tsp ground turmeric
1 tsp ground coriander
1 tsp ground cumin
125 g/4¹/₂ oz thick set
    natural yogurt
2 tsp gram flour or cornflour
¹/₂–1 tsp chilli powder
150 ml/5 fl oz warm water
1 tbsp chopped fresh mint leaves
2 tbsp chopped fresh coriander
    leaves
Indian bread, to serve

method

1 In a medium saucepan, heat the oil over a low heat and add the cinnamon, cardamom, cloves and bay leaves. Let them sizzle for 25–30 seconds, then add the meat, increase the heat to medium–high and cook until the meat begins to brown and all the natural juices have evaporated.

2 Add the onion and ginger and garlic purées, cook for 5–6 minutes, stirring regularly, then add the tomato purée, turmeric, ground coriander and cumin. Continue to cook for 3–4 minutes.

3 Whisk together the yogurt, gram flour and chilli powder and add to the meat. Reduce the heat to low, add the warm water, cover and simmer, stirring to ensure that the sauce does not stick to the base of the pan, for 45–50 minutes, or until the meat is tender. Simmer uncovered, if necessary, to thicken the sauce to a desired consistency.

4 Stir in the fresh mint and coriander, remove from the heat and serve with Indian bread.

lamb & spinach curry

ingredients

serves 2–4

300 ml/10 fl oz vegetable oil
2 onions, sliced
¼ bunch of fresh coriander
2 fresh green chillies, chopped
1½ tsp finely chopped fresh ginger
1½ tsp crushed fresh garlic
1 tsp chilli powder
½ tsp ground turmeric
450 g/1 lb lean lamb, cut into
    bite-sized chunks
1 tsp salt
1 kg/2 lb 4 oz fresh spinach,
    trimmed, washed and chopped
700 ml/1¼ pints water
finely chopped fresh red chilli,
    to garnish

method

1 Heat the oil in a large, heavy-based frying pan. Add the onions and cook until light golden.

2 Add the fresh coriander and green chillies to the frying pan and stir-fry for 3–5 minutes. Reduce the heat and add the ginger, garlic, chilli powder and turmeric, stirring well.

3 Add the lamb to the frying pan and stir-fry for a further 5 minutes. Add the salt and the spinach and cook, stirring occasionally with a wooden spoon, for a further 3–5 minutes.

4 Add the water, stirring, and cook over a low heat, covered, for 45 minutes. Remove the lid and check the meat. If it is not tender, turn the meat over, increase the heat and cook, uncovered, until the surplus water has been absorbed. Stir-fry the mixture for a further 5–7 minutes.

5 Transfer the lamb and spinach mixture to a serving dish and garnish with chopped red chilli. Serve hot.

meatballs in creamy cashew nut sauce

ingredients

serves 4

450 g/1 lb fresh lean lamb mince
1 tbsp thick set natural yogurt
1 egg, beaten
½ tsp ground cardamom
½ tsp ground nutmeg
½ tsp pepper
½ tsp dried mint
½ tsp salt, or to taste
300 ml/10 fl oz water
2.5-cm/1-inch piece cinnamon stick
5 green cardamom pods
5 cloves
2 bay leaves
3 tbsp sunflower or olive oil
1 onion, finely chopped
2 tsp garlic purée
1 tsp ground ginger
1 tsp ground fennel seeds
½ tsp ground turmeric
½ – 1 tsp chilli powder
125 g/4½ oz raw cashew nuts,
    soaked in boiling water
150 ml/5 fl oz double cream
1 tbsp crushed pistachio nuts,
    to garnish

method

1 Put the lamb mince in a mixing bowl and add the yogurt, egg, cardamom, nutmeg, pepper, mint and salt. Knead the mince until it is smooth and velvety. Chill for 30–40 minutes, then divide into quarters. Make five balls out of each quarter and roll them between your palms to make them smooth and neat.

2 Bring the 300 ml/10 fl oz water to the boil in a large shallow pan and add all the whole spices and the bay leaves. Arrange the meatballs in a single layer in the spiced liquid, reduce the heat, cover the pan and cook for 12–15 minutes. Remove the meatballs, cover and keep hot. Strain the spiced stock and set aside.

3 Wipe out the pan and add the oil. Place over a medium heat and add the onion and garlic purée. Add the ground ginger, ground fennel seeds, turmeric and chilli powder. Stir-fry for 2–3 minutes, then add the strained stock and meatballs. Bring to the boil, reduce the heat to low, cover and simmer for 10–12 minutes.

4 Meanwhile, purée the cashews in a blender and add to the meatball mixture along with the cream. Simmer for a further 5–6 minutes, then remove from the heat. Garnish with crushed pistachio nuts and serve.

lamb kebabs

ingredients

serves 8

55 g/2 oz raw cashew nuts
3 tbsp double cream
1 egg
1 tbsp gram flour
2 fresh green chillies, roughly
    chopped
2 shallots, roughly chopped
450 g/1 lb fresh lamb mince
1 tsp salt, or to taste
2 tsp garlic purée
2 tsp ginger purée
1 tsp ground cumin
1 tsp garam masala
1 tbsp chopped fresh mint leaves
2 tbsp chopped fresh coriander
    leaves
½ red pepper, deseeded and finely
    chopped
2 tbsp vegetable oil, for brushing
55 g/2 oz butter, melted
salad and chutney, to serve

method

1 Put the cashew nuts in a heatproof bowl, cover with boiling water and leave to soak for 20 minutes. Drain and put in a food processor. Add the cream and egg and process the ingredients to a coarse mixture.

2 Add all the remaining ingredients, except the herbs, red pepper, oil and butter, and process until thoroughly mixed. Transfer the mixture to a large bowl. Add the herbs and red pepper and mix well. Cover and chill in the refrigerator for 30–40 minutes.

3 Preheat the grill to high. Brush a grill rack and 8 metal skewers lightly with oil. Divide the chilled mixture into 8 equal-sized portions. Dip your hands into a bowl of cold water – this will stop the mixture sticking to your fingers when you are moulding it onto the skewers. Carefully mould each portion onto a skewer, forming it into a 15-cm/6-inch sausage shape. Arrange the kebabs on the prepared rack and cook under the preheated grill for 4 minutes. Brush with half the melted butter and cook for a further minute. Turn over and cook for 3 minutes. Baste with the remaining melted butter and cook for a further 2 minutes.

4 Remove from the heat and leave the kebabs to rest for 5 minutes before sliding them off the skewers with a knife. Serve with salad and chutney.

kashmiri lamb chops

ingredients

serves 4

4 lamb chump chops or
    8 cutlets
300 ml/10 fl oz full-fat milk
1 tbsp ginger purée
½ tsp pepper
pinch of saffron threads, pounded
1½ tsp ground fennel seeds
1 tsp ground cumin
½ tsp chilli powder
4 cloves
2.5-cm/1-inch piece
    cinnamon stick
4 green cardamom pods, bruised
1 tsp salt, or to taste
½ tsp garam masala
1 tbsp fresh mint leaves, chopped,
    or ½ tsp dried mint
1 tbsp chopped fresh
    coriander leaves
mixed leaf salad, to serve

method

1 Remove the rind from the chops. Bring enough water to cover the chops to the boil in a medium saucepan. Add the chops, return to the boil and cook for 2–3 minutes. Drain the chops, rinse and drain again.

2 Put the drained chops into a large non-stick saucepan and add all the remaining ingredients, except the garam masala and herbs. Place the saucepan over a medium heat and stir until the milk begins to bubble. Reduce the heat to low, cover and cook for 30 minutes, turning the chops occasionally.

3 Remove from the heat. Using tongs, lift the chops out of the saucepan and shake the cooking liquid back into the saucepan. Strain the liquid and return to the saucepan with the chops. Cook over a medium heat, turning frequently, for 7–8 minutes, until the liquid has evaporated and the chops are browned.

4 Sprinkle the garam masala evenly over the chops and add the mint and coriander. Stir and cook for 1 minute. Serve immediately with a mixed salad.

sesame lamb chops

ingredients

serves 4

12 lamb chops, such as best
    end of neck or middle neck
vegetable oil, for brushing
1½ tbsp sesame seeds
pepper
lime wedges, to serve

marinade

4 tbsp natural yogurt
2 tbsp grated lemon rind
1½ tsp ground cumin
1½ tsp ground coriander
¼ tsp chilli powder
salt

method

1 To make the marinade, put the yogurt, lemon rind,
    cumin, coriander, chilli powder and salt to taste in
    a large bowl and stir together.

2 Use a sharp knife to trim any fat from the edge of the
    lamb chops and scrape the meat off the long piece
    of bone. Using a rolling pin or the end of a large
    chef's knife, pound each chop until it is about 5mm/
    ¼ inch thick.

3 Add the chops to the bowl and use your hands to stir
    around until they are coated in the marinade. Leave to
    marinate for 20 minutes at room temperature, or cover
    the bowl and refrigerate for up to 4 hours. Return to
    room temperature before cooking.

4 Preheat the grill to its highest setting and brush the
    grill rack lightly with oil.

5 Arrange the chops on the grill rack in a single layer,
    then sprinkle the sesame seeds over each. Grill the
    chops about 10 cm/4 inches from the heat for about
    7 minutes, without turning, for medium.

6 Grind pepper over the chops and serve with lime
    wedges for squeezing over.

marinated lamb brochettes

ingredients

serves 4

700 g/1 lb 9 oz boned leg of lamb,
    cut into 2.5-cm/1-inch cubes
2 tbsp light malt vinegar
½ tsp salt, or to taste
1 tbsp garlic purée
1 tbsp ginger purée
115 g/4 oz whole milk natural
    yogurt, strained, or
    Greek-style yogurt
1 tbsp gram flour
1 tsp ground cumin
1 tsp garam masala
½–1 tsp chilli powder
½ tsp ground turmeric
3 tbsp olive or sunflower oil, plus
    1 tbsp for brushing
½ red pepper, deseeded and cut
    into 2.5-cm/1-inch pieces
½ green pepper, deseeded and cut
    into 2.5-cm/1-inch pieces
8 shallots, halved
55 g/2 oz butter, melted
lemon wedges, to serve

method

1 Put the meat in a large non-metallic bowl and add the vinegar, salt and garlic and ginger purées. Mix together thoroughly, cover and leave to marinate in the refrigerator for 30 minutes.

2 Put the yogurt and gram flour in a separate bowl and beat together with a fork until smooth. Add the cumin, garam masala, chilli powder, turmeric and oil and mix together thoroughly. Add the yogurt mixture to the marinated meat, then add the peppers and shallots and stir until well blended. Cover and leave to marinate in the refrigerator for 2–3 hours, or overnight. Return to room temperature before cooking.

3 Preheat the grill to high. Line the grill pan with a piece of foil. Brush the rack and 4 metal skewers with the oil. Thread the marinated lamb, peppers and shallots alternately onto the prepared skewers. Place the skewers on the prepared rack and cook under the preheated grill for 4 minutes. Brush generously with half the melted butter and cook for a further 2 minutes. Turn over and cook for 3–4 minutes. Brush with the remaining butter and cook for a further 2 minutes.

4 Balance the brochettes over a large saucepan or frying pan and leave to rest for 5–6 minutes before sliding off the skewers with a knife. Serve with the lemon wedges.

balti beef

ingredients

serves 4–6

30 g/1 oz ghee or 2 tbsp vegetable
    or groundnut oil
1 large onion, chopped
2 garlic cloves, crushed
2 large red peppers, deseeded
    and chopped
600 g/1 lb 5 oz boneless beef,
    such as sirloin, thinly sliced
fresh coriander sprigs,
    to garnish
Indian bread, to serve

balti sauce

30 g/1 oz ghee or 2 tbsp vegetable
    or groundnut oil
2 large onions, chopped
1 tbsp garlic and ginger paste
400 g/14 oz canned chopped
    tomatoes
1 tsp ground paprika
½ tsp ground turmeric
½ tsp ground cumin
½ tsp ground coriander
¼ tsp chilli powder
¼ tsp ground cardamom
1 bay leaf
salt and pepper

method

1 To make the balti sauce, melt the ghee in a wok or large frying pan over a medium–high heat. Add the onions and garlic and ginger paste and stir-fry for about 5 minutes, until the onions are golden brown. Stir in the tomatoes, then add the paprika, turmeric, cumin, coriander, chilli powder, cardamom, bay leaf and salt and pepper to taste. Bring to the boil, stirring, then reduce the heat and simmer for 20 minutes, stirring occasionally.

2 Leave the sauce to cool slightly, then remove the bay leaf and pour the mixture into a food processor or blender and whizz to a smooth sauce.

3 Wipe out the wok and return it to a medium–high heat. Add the ghee and melt. Add the onion and garlic and stir-fry for 5–8 minutes, until golden brown. Add the red peppers and continue stir-frying for 2 minutes.

4 Stir in the beef and continue stirring for 2 minutes, until it starts to turn brown. Add the balti sauce and bring to the boil. Reduce the heat and simmer for 5 minutes, or until the sauce slightly reduces again and the peppers are tender. Adjust the seasoning, if necessary. Garnish with coriander sprigs and serve with Indian bread.

beef madras

ingredients

serves 4-6

1–2 dried red chillies
2 tsp ground coriander
2 tsp ground turmeric
1 tsp black mustard seeds
½ tsp ground ginger
¼ tsp pepper
140 g/5 oz creamed coconut,
    grated, dissolved in 300 ml/
    10 fl oz boiling water
55 g/2 oz ghee or 4 tbsp vegetable
    or groundnut oil
2 onions, chopped
3 large garlic cloves, chopped
700 g/1 lb 9 oz lean stewing steak,
    such as chuck, trimmed and
    cut into 5-cm/2-inch cubes
250 ml/9 fl oz beef stock
lemon juice
salt
poppadoms, to serve

method

1 Depending on how hot you want this dish to be, chop the chillies with or without any seeds. The more seeds you include, the hotter the dish will be. Put the chopped chilli and any seeds in a small bowl with the coriander, turmeric, mustard seeds, ginger and pepper and stir in a little of the dissolved creamed coconut to make a thin paste.

2 Melt the ghee in a flameproof casserole or large frying pan with a tight-fitting lid over a medium–high heat. Add the onions and garlic and cook for 5–8 minutes, stirring frequently, until the onions are golden brown. Add the spice paste and stir around for 2 minutes, or until you can smell the aromas.

3 Add the meat and stock and bring to the boil. Reduce the heat to its lowest level, cover tightly and simmer for 1½ hours, or until the beef is tender. Check occasionally that the meat isn't catching on the base of the pan and stir in a little extra water or stock, if necessary.

4 Uncover the pan and stir in the remaining dissolved coconut cream with the lemon juice and salt to taste. Bring to the boil, stirring, then reduce the heat again and simmer, still uncovered, until the sauce reduces slightly. Serve with poppadoms.

beef korma with almonds

ingredients

serves 6

300 ml/10 fl oz vegetable oil
3 onions, finely chopped
1 kg/2 lb 4 oz lean beef, cubed
1½ tsp garam masala
1½ tsp ground coriander
1½ tsp finely chopped fresh ginger
1½ tsp crushed garlic
1 tsp salt
150 ml/5 fl oz natural yogurt
2 whole cloves
3 green cardamom pods
4 black peppercorns
600 ml/1 pint water
chapatis, to serve

to garnish

chopped blanched almonds
sliced fresh green chillies
chopped fresh coriander

method

1 Heat the oil in a large heavy-based frying pan. Add the onions and stir-fry for 8–10 minutes, until golden. Remove half of the onions and reserve.

2 Add the meat to the remaining onions in the frying pan and stir-fry for 5 minutes. Remove the frying pan from the heat.

3 Mix the garam masala, ground coriander, ginger, garlic, salt and yogurt together in a large bowl. Gradually add the meat to the yogurt and spice mixture and mix to coat the meat on all sides. Place the meat mixture in the frying pan, return to the heat, and stir-fry for 5–7 minutes, or until the mixture is nearly brown.

4 Add the cloves, cardamom pods and peppercorns. Add the water, reduce the heat, cover and simmer for 45–60 minutes. If the water has completely evaporated but the meat is still not tender enough, add another 300 ml/10 fl oz water and cook for a further 10–15 minutes, stirring occasionally.

5 Transfer to serving dishes and garnish with the reserved onions, chopped almonds, chillies and fresh coriander. Serve with chapatis.

pork vindaloo

ingredients

serves 4

2–6 dried red chillies, torn
5 cloves
2.5-cm/1-inch piece cinnamon
    stick, broken up
4 green cardamom pods
½ tsp black peppercorns
½ mace blade
¼ nutmeg, lightly crushed
1 tsp cumin seeds
1½ tsp coriander seeds
½ tsp fenugreek seeds
2 tsp garlic purée
1 tbsp ginger purée
3 tbsp cider or white wine vinegar
1 tbsp tamarind or ½ lime juice
700 g/1 lb 9 oz boneless leg
    of pork, cut into 2.5-cm/
    1-inch cubes
4 tbsp sunflower or olive oil,
    plus 2 tsp
2 large onions, finely chopped
250 ml/9 fl oz warm water,
    plus 4 tbsp
1 tsp salt, or to taste
1 tsp soft dark brown sugar
2 large garlic cloves, finely sliced
8–10 fresh or dried curry leaves

method

1 Grind the first 10 ingredients (all the spices) to a fine powder in a spice grinder. Transfer the ground spices to a bowl and add the garlic and ginger purées, vinegar and tamarind juice. Mix together to form a paste.

2 Put the pork in a large non-metallic bowl and rub about one quarter of the spice paste into the meat. Cover and leave to marinate in the refrigerator for 30–40 minutes.

3 Heat the 4 tablespoons of oil in a medium heavy-based saucepan over a medium heat, add the onions and cook, stirring frequently, for 8–10 minutes, until lightly browned. Add the remaining spice paste and cook, stirring constantly, for 5–6 minutes. Add 2 tablespoons of the warm water and cook until it evaporates. Repeat with another 2 tablespoons of water.

4 Add the marinated pork and cook over medium–high heat for 5–6 minutes. Add the salt, sugar and 250ml/ 9 fl oz warm water. Bring to the boil, then reduce the heat to low, cover and simmer for 50–55 minutes.

5 Meanwhile, heat the 2 teaspoons of oil in a small saucepan over a low heat. Add the sliced garlic and cook, stirring, until it begins to brown. Add the curry leaves and leave to sizzle for 15–20 seconds. Stir the garlic mixture into the vindaloo. Serve immediately.

pork with cinnamon & fenugreek

ingredients

serves 4

1 tsp ground coriander
1 tsp ground cumin
1 tsp chilli powder
1 tbsp dried fenugreek leaves
1 tsp ground fenugreek
150 ml/5 fl oz natural yogurt
450 g/1 lb diced pork fillet
4 tbsp ghee or vegetable oil
1 large onion, sliced
5-cm/2-inch piece fresh ginger, finely chopped
4 garlic cloves, finely chopped
1 cinnamon stick
6 green cardamom pods
6 whole cloves
2 bay leaves
175 ml/6 fl oz water
salt

method

1 Mix together the coriander, cumin, chilli powder, dried fenugreek, ground fenugreek and yogurt in a small bowl. Place the pork in a large, shallow non-metallic dish and add the spice mixture, turning well to coat. Cover with clingfilm and leave to marinate in the refrigerator for 30 minutes.

2 Melt the ghee in a large heavy-based saucepan. Cook the onion over a low heat, stirring occasionally, for 5 minutes, or until soft. Add the ginger, garlic, cinnamon stick, cardamom pods, cloves and bay leaves and cook, stirring constantly, for 2 minutes, or until the spices give off their aroma. Add the meat with its marinade and the water, and season to taste with salt. Bring to the boil, reduce the heat, cover and simmer for 30 minutes.

3 Transfer the meat mixture to a preheated wok or large heavy-based frying pan and cook over a low heat, stirring constantly, until dry and tender. If necessary, sprinkle occasionally with a little water to prevent it from sticking to the wok. Serve immediately.

red curry pork with peppers

ingredients

serves 4

2 tbsp vegetable or groundnut oil
1 onion, coarsely chopped
2 garlic cloves, chopped
450 g/1 lb pork fillet, thickly sliced
1 red pepper, deseeded and cut
    into squares
175 g/6 oz mushrooms, quartered
2 tbsp Thai red curry paste
115 g/4 oz creamed coconut,
    chopped
300 ml/10 fl oz pork or vegetable
    stock
2 tbsp Thai soy sauce
4 tomatoes, peeled, deseeded
    and chopped
handful of fresh coriander, chopped

method

1 Heat the oil in a wok or large frying pan and cook the onion and garlic for 1–2 minutes, until they are softened but not browned.

2 Add the pork slices and stir-fry for 2–3 minutes until browned all over. Add the pepper, mushrooms and curry paste.

3 Dissolve the coconut in the stock and add to the wok with the soy sauce. Bring to the boil and simmer for 4–5 minutes until the liquid has reduced and thickened.

4 Add the tomatoes and coriander and cook for 1–2 minutes before serving.

variation

Replace the mushrooms with 1 medium courgette, thinly sliced.

railway pork & vegetables

ingredients

serves 4–6

40 g/1½ oz ghee or 3 tbsp
    vegetable or groundnut oil
1 large onion, finely chopped
4 green cardamom pods
3 cloves
1 cinnamon stick
1 tbsp garlic and ginger paste
2 tsp garam masala
¼–½ tsp chilli powder
½ tsp ground asafoetida
2 tsp salt, or to taste
600 g/1 lb 5 oz fresh lean
    pork mince
1 potato, scrubbed and cut into
    5-mm/¼-inch dice
400 g/14 oz canned chopped
    tomatoes
125 ml/4 fl oz water
1 bay leaf
1 large carrot, coarsely grated
salt and pepper

method

1 Melt the ghee in a flameproof casserole or large frying
    pan with a tight-fitting lid over a medium heat. Add the
    onion and cook, stirring occasionally, for 5–8 minutes,
    until golden brown. Add the cardamom pods, cloves
    and cinnamon stick and cook, stirring, for 1 minute, or
    until you can smell the aromas.

2 Add the garlic and ginger paste, garam masala, chilli
    powder, asafoetida and salt and stir around for a further
    minute. Add the pork and cook for 5 minutes, or until no
    longer pink, using a wooden spoon to break up the meat.

3 Add the potato, tomatoes, water and bay leaf and
    bring to the boil, stirring. Reduce the heat to the lowest
    level, cover tightly and simmer for 15 minutes. Stir in
    the carrot and simmer for a further 5 minutes, or until
    the potato and carrot are tender. Taste and adjust the
    seasoning, adding salt and pepper if necessary, and serve.

fish & seafood

bengali-style fish

ingredients

serves 4–8

1 tsp ground turmeric
1 tsp salt
1 kg/2 lb 4 oz cod fillet, skinned
    and cut into pieces
6 tbsp mustard oil
4 fresh green chillies
1 tsp finely chopped fresh ginger
1 tsp crushed garlic
2 onions, finely chopped
2 tomatoes, finely chopped
450 ml/16 fl oz water
chopped fresh coriander,
    to garnish
Indian bread, to serve

method

1 Mix the turmeric and salt together in a small bowl, then spoon the mixture over the fish pieces.

2 Heat the mustard oil in a large heavy-based frying pan. Add the fish and fry until pale yellow. Remove the fish with a slotted spoon and reserve.

3 Place the chillies, ginger, garlic, onions and tomatoes in a mortar and grind with a pestle to make a paste. Alternatively, place the ingredients in a food processor and process until smooth.

4 Transfer the spice paste to a clean frying pan and dry-fry until golden brown.

5 Remove the frying pan from the heat and place the fish pieces in the paste without breaking up the fish. Return the frying pan to the heat, add the water and cook over a medium heat for 15–20 minutes. Transfer to a warmed serving dish, garnish with chopped coriander and serve with Indian bread.

steamed fish with coriander chutney

ingredients

serves 4

1 quantity of coriander chutney
    (see page 180)
1 large fresh banana leaf
vegetable or groundnut oil
4 white fish fillets, such as pomfret
    or sole, about 140 g/5 oz each
salt and pepper
lime or lemon wedges, to serve

method

1 Prepare the coriander chutney at least 2 hours in advance by blending the ingredients in a small food processor and allowing the flavours to blend.

2 Meanwhile, cut the banana leaf into 4 squares large enough to fold comfortably around the fish to make tight parcels. Working with one piece of leaf at a time, very lightly rub the bottom with oil. Put one of the fish fillets in the centre of the oiled side, flesh-side up. Spread one quarter of the coriander chutney over the top and season to taste with salt and pepper.

3 Fold one side of the leaf over the fish, then fold over the opposite side. Turn the leaf so the folded edges are top and bottom. Fold the right-hand end of the leaf parcel into the centre, then fold over the left-hand side. Trim the ends if the parcel becomes too bulky. Use 2 wooden skewers to close the leaf parcel. Repeat with the remaining ingredients and banana leaf squares.

4 Place a steamer large enough to hold the parcels in a single layer over a pan of boiling water. Add the fish, cover the pan and steam for 15 minutes. Make sure the fish is cooked through and flakes easily. Serve the fish parcels with lime or lemon wedges.

sole in chilli yogurt

ingredients

serves 4

2 tbsp vegetable or groundnut oil
1 large onion, sliced
4-cm/1½-inch piece fresh ginger,
    finely chopped
½ tsp salt
¼ tsp ground turmeric
pinch of ground cinnamon
pinch of ground cloves
200 ml/7 fl oz natural yogurt
1 tbsp plain flour
small pinch of chilli powder
4 skinless sole fillets, about
    150 g/5½ oz each, wiped dry
30 g/1 oz ghee or 2 tbsp vegetable
    or groundnut oil
salt and pepper
2 fresh fat green chillies, deseeded
    and finely chopped, to garnish

method

1 Heat the oil in a large frying pan over a medium–high heat. Add the onion and fry, stirring, for 8 minutes, or until it is soft and dark golden brown. Add the ginger and stir around for a further minute.

2 Stir in the salt, turmeric, cinnamon and cloves and continue stirring for 30 seconds. Remove the pan from the heat and stir in the yogurt, a little at a time, beating constantly.

3 Transfer the yogurt mixture to a blender or food processor and whizz until a paste forms.

4 Season the flour with chilli powder and salt and pepper to taste. Place it on a plate and use to dust the fish fillets lightly on both sides.

5 Wipe out the pan, then melt the ghee over a medium–high heat. When it is bubbling, reduce the heat to medium and add the fish fillets in a single layer. Fry for 2½ minutes, or until golden, then turn them over.

6 Continue frying for a further minute, then add the yogurt sauce to the pan and reheat, stirring. When the fillets flake easily and are cooked through and the sauce is hot, transfer to plates and sprinkle with the green chilli.

balti fish curry

ingredients

serves 4–6

900 g/2 lb thick fish fillets, such as
monkfish, grey mullet, cod or
haddock, rinsed and cut into
large chunks
2 bay leaves, torn
140 g/5 oz ghee or 150 ml/5 fl oz
vegetable or groundnut oil
2 large onions, chopped
½ tbsp salt
150 ml/5 fl oz water
chopped fresh coriander,
to garnish
Indian bread, to serve

marinade

½ tbsp garlic and ginger paste
1 fresh green chilli, deseeded and
chopped
1 tsp ground coriander
1 tsp ground cumin
½ tsp ground turmeric
¼–½ tsp chilli powder
1 tbsp water
salt

method

1 To make the marinade, mix the garlic and ginger paste,
green chilli, ground coriander, cumin, turmeric and
chilli powder together with salt to taste in a large bowl.
Gradually stir in the water to form a thin paste. Add
the fish chunks and smear with the marinade. Tuck
the bay leaves underneath and leave to marinate in
the refrigerator for at least 30 minutes, or up to 4 hours.

2 Remove the fish from the refrigerator 15 minutes in
advance of cooking. Melt the ghee in a wok or large
frying pan over a medium–high heat. Add the onions,
sprinkle with the salt and cook, stirring frequently, for
8 minutes, or until they are very soft and golden.

3 Gently add the fish with its marinade and the bay
leaves to the pan and stir in the water. Bring to the
boil, then immediately reduce the heat and cook the
fish for 4–5 minutes, spooning the sauce over the fish
and carefully moving the chunks around until they are
cooked through and the flesh flakes easily. Garnish
with coriander and serve with Indian bread.

goan-style seafood curry

ingredients

serves 4–6

3 tbsp vegetable or groundnut oil

1 tbsp black mustard seeds

12 fresh or 1 tbsp dried curry
    leaves

6 shallots, finely chopped

1 garlic clove, crushed

1 tsp ground turmeric

½ tsp ground coriander

¼–½ tsp chilli powder

140 g/5 oz creamed coconut,
    grated and dissolved in
    300 ml/10 fl oz boiling water

500 g/1 lb 2 oz skinless, boneless
    white fish, such as monkfish or
    cod, cut into large chunks

450 g/1 lb large raw prawns,
    peeled and deveined

finely grated rind and juice
    of 1 lime

salt

method

1 Heat the oil in a wok or large frying pan over a high heat. Add the mustard seeds and stir them around for about 1 minute, or until they pop. Stir in the curry leaves.

2 Add the shallots and garlic and stir for about 5 minutes, or until the shallots are golden. Stir in the turmeric, coriander and chilli powder and continue stirring for about 30 seconds. Add the dissolved creamed coconut. Bring to the boil, then reduce the heat to medium and stir for about 2 minutes.

3 Reduce the heat to low, add the fish and simmer for 1 minute, spooning the sauce over the fish and very gently stirring it around. Add the prawns and continue to simmer for a further 4–5 minutes, until the fish flakes easily and the prawns turn pink and curl.

4 Add half the lime juice, then taste and add more lime juice and salt to taste. Sprinkle with the lime rind and serve.

variation

Replace the mustard seeds with 2 teaspoons of dry mustard powder, which should be added to the pan with the turmeric.

fish in tomato & chilli sauce with fried onion

ingredients

serves 4

700 g/1 lb 9 oz tilapia fillets,
    cut into 5-cm/2-inch pieces
2 tbsp lemon juice
1 tsp salt, or to taste
1 tsp ground turmeric
4 tbsp sunflower or olive oil,
    plus extra for shallow-frying
2 tsp granulated sugar
1 large onion, finely chopped
2 tsp ginger purée
2 tsp garlic purée
$^1/_2$ tsp ground fennel seeds
1 tsp ground coriander
$^1/_2$–1 tsp chilli powder
175 g/6 oz canned chopped
    tomatoes
300 ml/10 fl oz warm water
2–3 tbsp chopped fresh
    coriander leaves
cooked basmati rice, to serve

method

1 Lay the fish on a plate and gently rub in the lemon juice, half the salt and half the turmeric. Set aside for 15–20 minutes. Pour enough oil to cover the base of a frying pan to a depth of about 1 cm/$^1/_2$ inch and place over a medium–high heat. Fry the pieces of fish, in a single layer, until well browned on both sides. Drain.

2 Heat the 4 tablespoons of oil in a medium saucepan over a medium heat and add the sugar. Allow it to brown, without blackening. Add the onion and cook for 5 minutes, until soft. Add the ginger and garlic purées, and cook for a further 3–4 minutes.

3 Add the ground fennel, ground coriander, chilli powder and the remaining turmeric. Cook for about a minute, then add half the tomatoes. Cook until the tomato juice has evaporated, then add the remaining tomatoes. Continue to cook, stirring, until the oil separates from the spice paste.

4 Pour in the warm water and add the remaining salt. Bring to the boil, then add the fish, stir gently, and reduce the heat to low. Cook, uncovered, for 5–6 minutes, then stir in the chopped coriander and remove from the heat. Serve with cooked basmati rice.

fish korma

ingredients

serves 4

700 g/1 lb 9 oz tilapia fillets,
   cut into 5-cm/2-inch pieces
1 tbsp lemon juice
1 tsp salt
55 g/2 oz raw unsalted cashews
3 tbsp sunflower or olive oil
5-cm/2-inch piece cinnamon stick,
   halved
4 green cardamom pods, bruised
2 cloves
1 large onion, finely chopped
1–2 fresh green chillies, chopped
   (deseeded if you like)
2 tsp ginger purée
2 tsp garlic purée
150 ml/5 fl oz single cream
55 g/2 oz whole milk natural
   yogurt
¼ tsp ground turmeric
½ tsp sugar
1 tbsp toasted flaked almonds,
   to garnish
Indian bread, to serve

method

1 Place the fish in a large plate and gently rub in the lemon juice and ½ teaspoon of the salt. Set aside for 20 minutes. Put the cashews in a bowl, cover with boiling water and leave to soak for 15 minutes.

2 Heat the oil in a wide shallow pan over a low heat and add the cinnamon, cardamom and cloves. Let them sizzle for 30–40 seconds.

3 Add the onion, chillies and ginger and garlic purées. Increase the heat slightly and cook, stirring frequently, for 9–10 minutes, until the onion is very soft.

4 Meanwhile, drain the cashews and purée them with the cream and yogurt.

5 Stir the turmeric into the onion mixture and add the puréed ingredients, the remaining salt and the sugar. Mix thoroughly and arrange the fish in the sauce in a single layer. Bring to a slow simmer, cover the pan and cook for 5 minutes. Remove the lid and shake the pan gently from side to side. Spoon some of the sauce over the pieces of fish. Re-cover and cook for a further 3–4 minutes.

6 Transfer to a serving dish and garnish with the toasted almonds. Serve with Indian bread.

fish tikka

ingredients

serves 8

pinch of saffron threads, pounded
1 tbsp hot milk
85 g/3 oz Greek-style yogurt
1 tbsp garlic purée
1 tbsp ginger purée
1 tsp salt, or to taste
$\frac{1}{2}$ tsp granulated sugar
juice of $\frac{1}{2}$ lemon
$\frac{1}{2}$ – 1 tsp chilli powder
$\frac{1}{2}$ tsp garam masala
1 tsp ground fennel seeds
2 tsp gram flour
750 g/1 lb 10 oz salmon fillets,
    skinned and cut into
    5-cm/2-inch cubes
3 tbsp olive oil, plus extra
    for brushing
sliced tomatoes and cucumber,
    to garnish
lemon wedges, to serve

method

1 Soak the pounded saffron in the hot milk for 10 minutes.

2 Put all the remaining ingredients, except the fish and oil, in a bowl and beat with a fork or a wire whisk until smooth. Stir in the saffron and milk, mix well and add the fish cubes. Using a metal spoon, mix gently, turning the fish around until fully coated with the marinade. Cover and leave to marinate in the refrigerator for 2 hours. Return to room temperature before cooking.

3 Preheat the grill to high. Brush a grill rack generously with oil and 8 metal skewers lightly with oil. Line the grill pan with a piece of foil.

4 Thread the fish cubes onto the prepared skewers, leaving a narrow gap between each piece. Arrange on the prepared rack and cook under the preheated grill for 3 minutes. Brush half the 3 tablespoons of oil over the kebabs and cook for a further minute. Turn over and brush any remaining marinade over the fish. Cook for 3 minutes. Brush the remaining oil over the fish and cook for a further 2 minutes, or until the fish is lightly charred.

5 Remove from the heat and leave to rest for 5 minutes. Garnish with tomatoes and cucumber and serve with lemon wedges for squeezing over.

mussels with mustard seeds & shallots

ingredients

serves 4

2 kg/4 lb 8 oz live mussels,
    scrubbed and debearded
3 tbsp vegetable or groundnut oil
½ tbsp black mustard seeds
8 shallots, chopped
2 garlic cloves, crushed
2 tbsp distilled vinegar
4 small fresh red chillies
85 g/3 oz creamed coconut,
    dissolved in 300 ml/
    10 fl oz boiling water
10 fresh or 1 tbsp dried
    curry leaves
½ tsp ground turmeric
¼–½ tsp chilli powder
salt

method

1 Discard any mussels with broken shells and any that refuse to close when tapped with a knife. Set aside.

2 Heat the oil in a wok or large frying pan over a medium–high heat. Add the mustard seeds and stir them around for about 1 minute, or until they start to pop.

3 Add the shallots and garlic and cook, stirring frequently, for 3 minutes, or until they start to brown. Stir in the vinegar, whole chillies, dissolved creamed coconut, curry leaves, turmeric, chilli powder and a pinch of salt and bring to the boil, stirring.

4 Reduce the heat to very low. Add the mussels, cover the pan and leave the mussels to simmer, shaking the pan frequently, for 3–4 minutes, or until they are all open. Discard any mussels that remain closed. Ladle the mussels into deep bowls, then taste the broth and add extra salt, if necessary. Spoon over the mussels and serve.

mussels in coconut sauce

ingredients

serves 4

1 kg/2 lb 4 oz live mussels, scrubbed and debearded
3 tbsp ghee or vegetable oil
1 onion, finely chopped
1 tsp garlic purée
1 tsp ginger purée
1 tsp ground cumin
1 tsp ground coriander
1/2 tsp ground turmeric
pinch of salt
600 ml/1 pint canned coconut milk
chopped fresh coriander, to garnish

method

1 Discard any mussels with broken shells and any that refuse to close when tapped with a knife. Set aside.

2 Heat the ghee in a large heavy-based frying pan. Add the onion and cook over a low heat, stirring occasionally, for 10 minutes, or until golden.

3 Add the garlic and ginger purées and cook, stirring constantly, for 2 minutes. Add the cumin, ground coriander, turmeric and salt and cook, stirring continuously, for a further 2 minutes. Stir in the coconut milk and bring to the boil.

4 Add the mussels, cover and cook for 5 minutes, or until the mussels have opened. Discard any mussels that remain closed. Transfer the mussels, with the coconut sauce, to a large warmed serving dish. Sprinkle with chopped coriander and serve immediately.

prawn and pineapple tikka

ingredients

serves 4

1 tsp cumin seeds
1 tsp coriander seeds
½ tsp fennel seeds
½ tsp yellow mustard seeds
¼ tsp fenugreek seeds
¼ tsp nigella seeds
pinch of chilli powder
2 tbsp lemon or pineapple juice
12 raw tiger prawns, peeled,
    deveined and tails left intact
12 bite-sized wedges of fresh or
    well-drained canned pineapple
salt
chopped fresh coriander,
    to garnish

method

1 Dry-roast the cumin, coriander, fennel, mustard, fenugreek and nigella seeds in a hot frying pan over a high heat, stirring them around constantly, until you can smell the aroma of the spices. Immediately tip the spices out of the pan so they do not burn, and reserve.

2 Put the spices in a spice grinder or mortar, add the chilli powder and salt to taste and grind to a fine powder. Transfer to a non-metallic bowl and stir in the lemon juice.

3 Add the prawns to the bowl and stir them around so they are well coated, then set aside to marinate for 10 minutes. Meanwhile, preheat the grill to high.

4 Thread 3 prawns and 3 pineapple wedges alternately onto metal or presoaked wooden skewers. Grill about 10 cm/4 inches from the heat for 2 minutes on each side, brushing with any leftover marinade, until the prawns turn pink and are cooked through.

5 Serve the prawns and pineapple wedges on the skewers with plenty of fresh coriander sprinkled over.

prawn pooris

ingredients

serves 6

2 tsp coriander seeds
½ tsp black peppercorns
1 large garlic clove, crushed
1 tsp ground turmeric
¼–½ tsp chilli powder
½ tsp salt
40 g/1½ oz ghee or 3 tbsp
    vegetable or groundnut oil
1 onion, grated
800 g/1 lb 12 oz canned
    crushed tomatoes
pinch of sugar
500 g/1 lb 2 oz small cooked
    peeled prawns, thawed
    if frozen
½ tsp garam masala, plus extra
    to garnish
6 pooris, kept warm
fresh chopped coriander, to garnish

method

1 Put the coriander seeds, peppercorns, garlic, turmeric, chilli powder and salt in a small food processor, spice grinder or mortar and blend to a thick paste.

2 Melt the ghee in a wok or large frying pan over a medium–low heat. Add the paste and cook, stirring constantly, for about 30 seconds.

3 Add the grated onion and stir around for a further 30 seconds. Stir in the tomatoes and the sugar. Bring to the boil, stirring, and leave to bubble for 10 minutes, or until reduced, mashing the tomatoes against the side of the pan to break them down. Taste and add extra salt, if necessary.

4 Add the prawns and sprinkle with the garam masala. When the prawns are hot, arrange the warm pooris on plates and top each one with a portion of the prawns. Sprinkle with the coriander and garam masala and serve.

prawns in coconut milk with chillies & curry leaves

ingredients

serves 4

4 tbsp sunflower or olive oil
½ tsp black or brown
    mustard seeds
½ tsp fenugreek seeds
1 large onion, finely chopped
2 tsp garlic purée
2 tsp ginger purée
1–2 fresh green chillies, chopped
    (deseeded if you like)
1 tbsp ground coriander
½ tsp ground turmeric
½ tsp chilli powder
1 tsp salt, or to taste
250 ml/9 fl oz canned
    coconut milk
450 g/1 lb cooked peeled tiger
    prawns, thawed and drained
    if frozen
1 tbsp tamarind juice or
    juice of ½ lime
½ tsp crushed black pepper
10–12 fresh or dried curry leaves

method

1 Heat 3 tablespoons of the oil in a medium saucepan over a medium–high heat. When hot, but not smoking, add the mustard seeds, followed by the fenugreek seeds and the onion. Cook, stirring frequently, for 5–6 minutes, until the onion is soft but not brown. Add the garlic and ginger purées and the chillies and cook, stirring frequently, for a further 5–6 minutes, until the onion is a light golden colour.

2 Add the coriander, turmeric and chilli powder and cook, stirring, for 1 minute. Add the salt and coconut milk, followed by the prawns and tamarind juice. Bring to a slow simmer and cook, stirring occasionally, for 3–4 minutes.

3 Meanwhile, heat the remaining oil in a very small saucepan over a medium heat. Add the pepper and curry leaves. Turn off the heat and leave to sizzle for 20–25 seconds, then fold the aromatic oil into the prawn mixture. Remove from the heat and serve immediately.

tandoori prawns

ingredients

serves 4

4 tbsp natural yogurt
2 fresh green chillies, deseeded
    and chopped
½ tbsp garlic and ginger paste
seeds from 4 green cardamom
    pods
2 tsp ground cumin
1 tsp tomato purée
¼ tsp ground turmeric
¼ tsp salt
pinch of chilli powder, ideally
    Kashmiri chilli powder
24 raw tiger prawns, thawed if
    frozen, peeled, deveined and
    tails left intact
oil, for greasing
lemon or lime wedges, to serve

method

1 Put the yogurt, chillies and garlic and ginger paste in
   a small food processor or spice grinder and whizz until
   a paste forms. Transfer the paste to a large non-metallic
   bowl and stir in the cardamom seeds, cumin, tomato
   purée, turmeric, salt and chilli powder.

2 Add the prawns to the bowl and use your hands to
   make sure they are coated with the yogurt marinade.
   Cover the bowl with clingfilm and chill for at least
   30 minutes, or up to 4 hours.

3 When you are ready to cook, heat a large griddle or
   frying pan over a high heat until a few drops of water
   'dance' when they hit the surface. Use crumpled
   kitchen paper or a pastry brush to grease the hot
   pan very lightly with oil.

4 Use tongs to lift the prawns out of the marinade,
   letting the excess drip back into the bowl, then place
   the prawns on the griddle and cook for 2 minutes. Flip
   the prawns over and cook for a further 1–2 minutes,
   until they turn pink, curl and are opaque all the way
   through when you cut one. Serve immediately with
   lemon or lime wedges for squeezing over.

vegetables
& pulses

mushroom bhaji

ingredients

serves 4

280 g/10 oz closed-cup white
    mushrooms
4 tbsp sunflower or olive oil
1 onion, finely chopped
1 fresh green chilli, finely chopped
    (deseeded if you like)
2 tsp garlic purée
1 tsp ground cumin
1 tsp ground coriander
½ tsp chilli powder
½ tsp salt, or to taste
1 tbsp tomato purée
3 tbsp water
1 tbsp snipped fresh chives,
    to garnish

method

1 Wipe the mushrooms with damp kitchen paper and thickly slice.

2 Heat the oil in a medium saucepan over a medium heat. Add the onion and chilli and cook, stirring frequently, for 5–6 minutes, until the onion is soft but not brown. Add the garlic purée and cook, stirring, for 2 minutes.

3 Add the cumin, coriander and chilli powder and cook, stirring, for 1 minute. Add the mushrooms, salt and tomato purée and stir until all the ingredients are thoroughly blended.

4 Sprinkle the water evenly over the mushrooms and reduce the heat to low. Cover and cook for 5 minutes, stir, then cook for a further 5 minutes. The sauce should have thickened, but if it appears runny, cook, uncovered, for 3–4 minutes, or until you achieve the desired consistency.

5 Transfer to a serving dish, sprinkle the chives on top and serve immediately.

vegetable korma

ingredients

serves 4

85 g/3 oz raw cashew nuts, soaked in boiling water

175 ml/6 fl oz boiling water

good pinch of saffron threads, soaked in 2 tbsp hot milk

1 small cauliflower, divided into 1-cm/½-inch florets

115 g/4 oz green beans, cut into 2.5-cm/1-inch lengths

115 g/4 oz carrots, cut into 2.5-cm/1-inch sticks

4 tbsp sunflower or olive oil

1 large onion, finely chopped

2 tsp ginger purée

1–2 fresh green chillies, chopped (deseeded if you like)

2 tsp ground coriander

½ tsp ground turmeric

6 tbsp warm water

400 ml/14 fl oz vegetable stock

½ tsp salt, or to taste

250 g/9 oz new potatoes, boiled in their skins and cooled, halved

2 tbsp single cream

2 tsp ghee or butter

1 tsp garam masala

¼ tsp grated nutmeg

method

1 Soak the cashew nuts and saffron threads. Blanch the vegetables in a saucepan of boiling salted water, then drain and immediately plunge in cold water. The cauliflower and green beans should each be blanched for 3 minutes, whilst carrots will need 4 minutes.

2 Heat the oil in a medium heavy-based saucepan over a medium heat. Add the onion, ginger purée and chillies and cook, stirring frequently, for 5–6 minutes, until the onion is soft. Add the coriander and turmeric and cook, stirring, for 1 minute. Add half the warm water and cook for 2–3 minutes. Repeat this process, then cook, stirring frequently, for 2–3 minutes, or until the oil separates from the spice paste.

3 Add the stock, saffron and milk mixture and salt, and bring to the boil. Drain the vegetables, add to the saucepan with the potatoes and return to the boil. Reduce the heat to low and simmer for 2–3 minutes. Meanwhile, put the cashew nuts and their soaking water in a food processor and process until well blended. Add to the korma, then stir in the cream.

4 Melt the ghee in a small saucepan over a low heat. Add the garam masala and nutmeg and sizzle gently for 20–25 seconds. Fold the spiced butter into the korma. Remove from the heat and serve.

cauliflower, aubergine & green bean korma

ingredients

serves 4–6

85 g/3 oz cashew nuts
1½ tbsp garlic and ginger paste
200 ml/7 fl oz water
55 g/2 oz ghee or 4 tbsp
    vegetable or groundnut oil
1 large onion, chopped
5 green cardamom pods, bruised
1 cinnamon stick, broken in half
½ tsp ground turmeric
250 ml/9 fl oz double cream
140 g/5 oz new potatoes,
    scrubbed and chopped into
    1-cm/½-inch pieces
140 g/5 oz cauliflower florets
½ tsp garam masala
140 g/5 oz aubergine, chopped
    into 2.5-cm/1-inch chunks
140 g/5 oz green beans, chopped
    into 2.5-cm/1-inch lengths
salt and pepper
chopped fresh mint, to garnish

method

1 Heat a large flameproof casserole over a high heat. Add the cashew nuts and stir them around until they start to brown, then tip them out of the casserole.

2 Put the nuts in a spice grinder with the garlic and ginger paste and 1 tablespoon of the water and whizz until a coarse paste forms.

3 Melt half the ghee in the casserole over a medium–high heat. Add the onion and cook for 5–8 minutes, until golden brown. Add the nut paste and stir for 5 minutes. Stir in the cardamom pods, cinnamon stick and turmeric.

4 Add the cream and the remaining water and bring to the boil, stirring. Reduce the heat to very low, cover and simmer for 5 minutes.

5 Add the potatoes, cauliflower and garam masala and simmer, covered, for 5 minutes. Stir in the aubergine and green beans and simmer until all the vegetables are tender. Check the sauce occasionally to make sure it isn't sticking, and stir in a little water if needed.

6 Taste and add seasoning, if necessary. Sprinkle with the mint and serve.

cauliflower & sweet potato curry

ingredients

serves 4

4 tbsp ghee or vegetable oil
2 onions, finely chopped
1 tsp panch phoran
1 cauliflower, broken into
    small florets
350 g/12 oz sweet potatoes, diced
2 fresh green chillies, deseeded
    and finely chopped
1 tsp ginger purée
2 tsp paprika
1½ tsp ground cumin
1 tsp ground turmeric
½ tsp chilli powder
3 tomatoes, quartered
225 g/8 oz fresh or frozen peas
3 tbsp natural yogurt
225 ml/8 fl oz vegetable stock
    or water
1 tsp garam masala
salt
fresh coriander sprigs,
    to garnish

method

1 Heat the ghee in a large heavy-based frying pan. Add the onions and panch phoran and cook over a low heat, stirring frequently, for 10 minutes, or until the onions are golden. Add the cauliflower, sweet potatoes and chillies and cook, stirring frequently, for 3 minutes.

2 Stir in the ginger purée, paprika, cumin, turmeric and chilli powder and cook, stirring constantly, for 3 minutes. Add the tomatoes and peas and stir in the yogurt and stock. Season with salt to taste, cover and simmer for 20 minutes, or until the vegetables are tender.

3 Sprinkle over the garam masala and transfer to a warmed serving dish. Garnish with coriander sprigs and serve immediately.

variation

Replace the peas with French beans, cut into small pieces.

cumin-scented aubergine & potato curry

ingredients

serves 4

1 large aubergine, about
   350 g/12 oz
225 g/8 oz potatoes, boiled in
   their skins and cooled
3 tbsp sunflower or olive oil
½ tsp black mustard seeds
½ tsp nigella seeds
½ tsp fennel seeds
1 onion, finely chopped
2.5-cm/1-inch piece fresh
   ginger, grated
2 fresh green chillies, chopped
   (deseeded if you like)
½ tsp ground cumin
1 tsp ground coriander
1 tsp ground turmeric
½ tsp chilli powder
1 tbsp tomato purée
450 ml/15 fl oz warm water
1 tsp salt, or to taste
½ tsp garam masala
2 tbsp chopped fresh
   coriander leaves
Indian bread, to serve

method

1 Quarter the aubergine lengthways and cut the stem
   end of each quarter into 5-cm/2-inch pieces. Halve the
   remaining part of each quarter and cut into the same
   size as above. Soak the aubergine pieces in cold water.

2 Peel the potatoes and cut into into 5-cm/2-inch cubes.
   Set aside. Heat the oil in a large saucepan over a
   medium heat. When hot, add the mustard seeds and,
   as soon as they start popping, add the nigella seeds
   and fennel seeds.

3 Add the onion, ginger and chillies and cook for
   7–8 minutes, until the mixture begins to brown.
   Add the cumin, coriander, turmeric and chilli powder.
   Cook for about a minute, then add the tomato purée.
   Cook for a further minute, pour in the warm water,
   then add the salt and aubergine. Bring to the boil and
   cook over a medium heat for 8–10 minutes, stirring
   frequently. At the start of cooking, the aubergine will
   float, but once it soaks up the liquid it will sink quite
   quickly. When the aubergine sinks, add the potatoes
   and cook for a further 2–3 minutes, stirring.

4 Stir in the garam masala and chopped coriander
   and remove from the heat. Serve with Indian bread.

tofu & vegetable curry

ingredients

serves 4

vegetable or groundnut oil,
    for deep-frying
225 g/8 oz firm tofu, drained
    and cut into cubes
2 tbsp vegetable or groundnut oil
2 onions, chopped
2 garlic cloves, chopped
1 fresh red chilli, deseeded
    and sliced
3 celery sticks, diagonally sliced
225 g/8 oz mushrooms, thickly
    sliced
115 g/4 oz baby corn cobs,
    cut in half
1 red pepper, deseeded and cut
    into strips
3 tbsp Thai red curry paste
400 ml/14 fl oz coconut milk
1 tsp palm sugar or soft, light
    brown sugar
2 tbsp Thai soy sauce
225 g/8 oz baby spinach leaves

method

1 Heat the oil for deep-frying in a preheated wok or a deep saucepan or deep-fat fryer to 180–190°C/350–375°F, or until a cube of bread browns in 30 seconds. Add the tofu cubes, in batches, and cook for 4–5 minutes until crisp and brown all over. Remove with a slotted spoon and drain on kitchen paper.

2 Heat the 2 tablespoons of oil in a wok or frying pan and stir-fry the onions, garlic and chilli for 1–2 minutes, until they start to soften. Add the celery, mushrooms, corn cobs and red pepper and stir-fry for 3–4 minutes, until they soften.

3 Stir in the curry paste and coconut milk and gradually bring to the boil. Add the sugar and soy sauce and then the spinach. Cook, stirring constantly, until the spinach has wilted. Serve immediately, topped with the tofu.

green bean and potato curry

ingredients

serves 6

300 ml/10 fl oz vegetable oil
1 tsp white cumin seeds
1 tsp mixed mustard and
  onion seeds
4 dried red chillies
3 fresh tomatoes, sliced
1 tsp salt
1 tsp fresh ginger, finely chopped
1 tsp crushed fresh garlic
1 tsp chilli powder
200 g/7 oz green beans, diagonally
  sliced into 2.5-cm/
  1-inch pieces
2 potatoes, peeled and diced
300 ml/10 fl oz water
chopped fresh coriander and finely
  sliced green chillies, to garnish

method

1 Heat the oil in a large, heavy-based saucepan. Add the white cumin seeds, mustard and onion seeds and dried red chillies, stirring well.

2 Add the tomatoes to the pan and stir-fry the mixture for 3–5 minutes.

3 Mix together the salt, ginger, garlic and chilli powder in a bowl and spoon into the saucepan. Blend the whole mixture together.

4 Add the green beans and potatoes to the saucepan and stir-fry for 5 minutes.

5 Add the water to the saucepan, reduce the heat and simmer for 10–15 minutes, stirring occasionally. Transfer to a warmed serving dish, garnish with chopped coriander and green chillies and serve.

vegetable sambar

ingredients

serves 6

800 g/1 lb 12 oz canned tomatoes
2 tbsp desiccated coconut
2 tbsp lemon juice
1 tbsp yellow mustard seeds
40 g/1½ oz raw or muscovado
    sugar
2 tbsp ghee or vegetable oil
2 onions, sliced
4 cardamom pods, lightly crushed
6 curry leaves, plus extra to garnish
2 tsp ground coriander
2 tsp ground cumin
1 tsp ground turmeric
1 tsp ginger purée
200 g/7 oz toor dhal
450 g/1 lb sweet potatoes,
    cut into chunks
900 g/2 lb potatoes,
    cut into chunks
2 carrots, sliced
2 courgettes, cut into chunks
1 aubergine, cut into chunks
salt

method

1 Place the tomatoes and their can juices, the coconut, 1 tablespoon of the lemon juice, the mustard seeds and sugar in a food processor or blender and process until smooth.

2 Heat the ghee in a large, heavy-based saucepan. Add the onion and cook over a low heat, stirring occasionally, for 10 minutes, or until golden. Add the cardamom pods, curry leaves, coriander, cumin, turmeric and ginger purée and cook, stirring constantly, for 1–2 minutes, or until the spices give off their aroma.

3 Stir in the tomato mixture and dhal and bring to the boil. Reduce the heat, cover and simmer for 10 minutes.

4 Add the sweet potatoes, potatoes and carrots, re-cover the saucepan and simmer for a further 15 minutes. Add the courgettes, aubergine and remaining lemon juice, add salt to taste, re-cover and simmer for a further 10–15 minutes, or until the vegetables are tender. Serve garnished with curry leaves.

okra stir-fried with onions

ingredients

serves 4

280 g/10 oz okra
1 small red pepper
1 onion
2 tbsp sunflower or olive oil
1 tsp black or brown
    mustard seeds
½ tsp cumin seeds
3 large garlic cloves, lightly
    crushed, then chopped
½ tsp chilli powder
½ tsp salt, or to taste
½ tsp garam masala
cooked basmati rice,
    to serve

method

1 Scrub each okra gently, rinse well in cold running water, then slice off the hard head. Halve diagonally and set aside.

2 Remove the seeds and core from the red pepper and cut into 4-cm/1½-inch strips. Halve the onion lengthways and cut into 5-mm/¼-inch thick slices.

3 Heat the oil in a heavy-based frying pan or wok over a medium heat. When hot, but not smoking, add the mustard seeds, followed by the cumin seeds. Remove from the heat and add the garlic. Return to a low heat and cook the garlic gently, stirring, for 1 minute, or until lightly browned.

4 Add the okra, red pepper and onion, increase the heat to medium–high and stir-fry for 2 minutes. Add the chilli powder and salt and stir-fry for a further 3 minutes. Add the garam masala and stir-fry for 1 minute. Remove from the heat and serve at once with cooked basmati rice.

garlic & chilli-flavoured potatoes with cauliflower

ingredients

serves 4

350 g/12 oz new potatoes
1 small cauliflower
2 tbsp sunflower or olive oil
1 tsp black or brown mustard
    seeds
1 tsp cumin seeds
5 large garlic cloves, lightly
    crushed, then chopped
1–2 fresh green chillies, finely
    chopped (deseeded if you like)
$^1/_2$ tsp ground turmeric
$^1/_2$ tsp salt, or to taste
2 tbsp chopped fresh coriander
    leaves

method

1 Cook the potatoes in their skins in a saucepan of boiling water for 20 minutes, or until tender. Drain, then soak in cold water for 30 minutes. Peel them, if you like, then halve or quarter according to their size – they should be only slightly bigger than the size of the cauliflower florets.

2 Meanwhile, divide the cauliflower into about 1-cm/$^1/_2$-inch florets and blanch in a large saucepan of boiling salted water for 3 minutes. Drain and plunge into iced water to prevent further cooking, then drain again.

3 Heat the oil in a medium saucepan over a medium heat. When hot, but not smoking, add the mustard seeds, then the cumin seeds. Remove from the heat and add the garlic and chillies. Return to a low heat and cook, stirring, until the garlic has a light brown tinge.

4 Stir in the turmeric, followed by the cauliflower and the potatoes. Add the salt, increase the heat slightly and cook, stirring, until the vegetables are well blended with the spices and heated through.

5 Stir in the coriander, remove from the heat and serve immediately.

peas & paneer in chilli-tomato sauce

ingredients

serves 4

4 tbsp sunflower or olive oil
250 g/9 oz paneer, cut into
    2.5-cm/1-inch cubes
4 green cardamom pods, bruised
2 bay leaves
1 onion, finely chopped
2 tsp garlic purée
2 tsp ginger purée
2 tsp ground coriander
½ tsp ground turmeric
½–1 tsp chilli powder
150 g/5½ oz canned chopped
    tomatoes
425 ml/15 fl oz warm water,
    plus 2 tbsp
1 tsp salt, or to taste
125 g/4½ oz frozen peas
½ tsp garam masala
2 tbsp single cream
2 tbsp chopped fresh coriander
    leaves

method

1 Heat 2 tablespoons of the oil in a medium non-stick saucepan over a medium heat. Add the paneer and cook, stirring frequently, for 3–4 minutes, or until evenly browned. Remove and drain on kitchen paper.

2 Add the remaining oil to the saucepan and reduce the heat to low. Add the cardamom pods and bay leaves and leave to sizzle gently for 20–25 seconds. Add the onion, increase the heat to medium and cook, stirring frequently, for 4–5 minutes, until the onion is soft. Add the garlic and ginger purées and cook, stirring frequently, until the onion is a pale golden colour.

3 Add the ground coriander, turmeric and chilli powder and cook, stirring, for 1 minute. Add the tomatoes and cook, stirring, for 4–5 minutes. Add the 2 tablespoons of warm water and cook, stirring, for 3 minutes, or until the oil separates from the spice paste.

4 Add the 425 ml/15 fl oz of warm water and the salt. Bring to the boil, then simmer, uncovered, for 7–8 minutes. Add the paneer and peas and simmer for 5 minutes. Stir in the garam masala, cream and fresh coriander and remove from the heat. Serve immediately.

spinach & paneer

ingredients

serves 4

85 g/3 oz ghee or 6 tbsp vegetable or groundnut oil

350 g/12 oz paneer, cut into 1-cm/½-inch pieces

1½ tbsp garlic and ginger purée

1 fresh green chilli, chopped

4 tbsp water

1 onion, finely chopped

600 g/1 lb 5 oz fresh spinach leaves, rinsed and any thick stems removed and rinsed

¼ tsp salt

¼ tsp garam masala

4 tbsp double cream

lemon wedges, to serve

method

1 Melt the ghee in a flameproof casserole or large frying pan with a tight-fitting lid over a medium–high heat. Add as many paneer pieces as will fit in a single layer without overcrowding the casserole and fry for about 5 minutes until golden brown on all sides. Use a slotted spoon to remove the paneer and drain it on crumpled kitchen paper. Continue, adding a little extra ghee, if necessary, until all the paneer is fried.

2 Put the garlic and ginger purée and chilli in a spice grinder or pestle and mortar and grind until a thick paste forms. Add the water and blend again.

3 Reheat the casserole. Stir in the onion with the garlic and ginger purée mixture and fry, stirring frequently, for 5–8 minutes until the onion is soft, but not brown.

4 Add the spinach, with just the water clinging to the leaves, and the salt, and stir until it wilts. Reduce the heat to low, cover the casserole and continue simmering until the spinach is soft.

5 Stir in the garam masala and cream, then gently return the paneer to the casserole. Simmer, stirring gently, until the paneer is heated through. Taste and adjust the seasoning, if necessary. Serve with lemon wedges for squeezing over.

bombay potatoes

ingredients

serves 6

500 g/1 lb 2 oz new potatoes,
    halved
1 tsp ground turmeric
4 tbsp ghee or vegetable oil
6 curry leaves
1 dried red chilli
2 fresh green chillies, chopped
½ tsp nigella seeds
1 tsp mixed mustard and
    onion seeds
½ tsp cumin seeds
½ tsp fennel seeds
¼ tsp asafoetida
2 onions, chopped
5 tbsp chopped fresh coriander
juice of ½ lime
salt

method

1 Place the potatoes in a large, heavy-based saucepan
   and pour in just enough cold water to cover. Add
   ½ teaspoon of the turmeric and a pinch of salt and
   bring to the boil. Simmer for 10 minutes, or until tender,
   then drain and reserve until required.

2 Heat the ghee in a large, heavy-based frying pan. Add
   the curry leaves and dried red chilli and cook, stirring
   frequently, for a few minutes, or until the chilli is
   blackened. Add the remaining turmeric, the fresh
   chillies, the nigella, mustard and onion seeds, cumin
   and fennel seeds, the asafoetida, onions and fresh
   coriander and cook, stirring constantly, for 5 minutes,
   or until the onions have softened.

3 Stir in the potatoes and cook over a low heat, stirring
   frequently, for 10 minutes, or until heated through.
   Squeeze over the lime juice and serve.

potatoes with spiced spinach

ingredients

serves 4

350 g/12 oz new potatoes
250 g/9 oz spinach leaves,
    thawed if frozen
3 tbsp sunflower or olive oil
1 large onion, finely sliced
1 fresh green chilli, finely chopped
2 tsp garlic purée
2 tsp ginger purée
1 tsp ground coriander
½ tsp ground cumin
½ tsp chilli powder
½ tsp ground turmeric
200 g/7 oz canned chopped
    tomatoes
½ tsp granulated sugar
1 tsp salt, or to taste
3 tbsp single cream

method

1 Cook the potatoes in their skins in a saucepan of boiling water for 20 minutes, or until tender. Drain, then soak in cold water for 30 minutes. Peel them, if preferred, then halve or quarter.

2 Meanwhile, cook the spinach in a saucepan of boiling water for 2 minutes, then drain. Transfer to a food processor and blend to a purée.

3 Heat 2 tablespoons of the oil in a medium saucepan over a medium heat. Add the onion and cook, stirring, for 10–12 minutes, until browned, reducing the heat to low for the last 2–3 minutes. Remove from the heat and remove the excess oil from the onion. Drain on kitchen paper.

4 Return the pan to a low heat and add the remaining oil. Add the chilli and garlic and ginger purées and cook over a low heat, stirring, for 2–3 minutes. Add the coriander, cumin, chilli powder and turmeric and cook, stirring, for 1 minute. Add the tomatoes, increase the heat to medium and add the sugar. Cook, stirring, for 5–6 minutes.

5 Add the potatoes, spinach, salt and reserved onion and cook, stirring, for 2–3 minutes. Stir in the cream and cook for 1 minute. Remove from the heat and serve immediately.

chickpeas in coconut milk

ingredients

serves 4

275 g/9¾ oz potatoes, cut into
   1-cm/½-inch cubes
250 ml/9 fl oz hot water
400 g/14 oz canned chickpeas,
   drained and well rinsed
250 ml/9 fl oz canned
   coconut milk
1 tsp salt, or to taste
2 tbsp sunflower or olive oil
4 large garlic cloves, finely
   chopped or crushed
2 tsp ground coriander
½ tsp ground turmeric
½–1 tsp chilli powder
juice of ½ lemon
Indian bread, to serve

method

1 Put the potatoes in a medium saucepan and pour in the hot water. Bring to the boil, then reduce the heat to low and cook, covered, for 6–7 minutes, until the potatoes are al dente. Add the chickpeas and cook, uncovered, for 3–4 minutes, until the potatoes are tender. Add the coconut milk and salt and bring to a slow simmer.

2 Meanwhile, heat the oil in a small saucepan over a low heat. Add the garlic and cook, stirring frequently, until it begins to brown. Add the coriander, turmeric and chilli powder and cook, stirring, for 25–30 seconds.

3 Fold the aromatic oil into the chickpea mixture. Stir in the lemon juice and remove from the heat. Serve immediately with Indian bread.

chickpeas with spiced tomatoes

ingredients

serves 4

6 tbsp vegetable or groundnut oil

2 tsp cumin seeds

3 large onions, finely chopped

2 tsp garlic and ginger paste

2 small fresh green chillies, deseeded and thinly sliced

1½ tsp amchoor (dried mango powder)

1½ tsp garam masala

¾ tsp ground asafoetida

½ tsp ground turmeric

¼–1 tsp chilli powder

3 large, firm tomatoes, about 450 g/1 lb, grated

800 g/1 lb 12 oz canned chickpeas, rinsed and drained

6 tbsp water

300 g/10½ oz fresh spinach leaves, rinsed

½ tsp salt, or to taste

method

1 Heat the oil in a wok or large frying pan over a medium–high heat. Add the cumin seeds and stir around for 30 seconds, or until they brown and crackle, watching carefully because they can burn quickly.

2 Immediately stir in the onions, garlic and ginger paste and chillies and fry, stirring frequently, for 5–8 minutes, until the onions are golden.

3 Stir in the amchoor, garam masala, asafoetida, turmeric and chilli powder. Add the tomatoes to the pan, stir them around and continue frying, stirring frequently, until the sauce blends together and starts to brown slightly.

4 Stir in the chickpeas and water and bring to the boil. Reduce the heat to very low and use a wooden spoon or a potato masher to mash about a quarter of the chickpeas, leaving the remainder whole.

5 Add the spinach to the pan with just the water clinging to the leaves and stir around until it wilts and is cooked. Stir in the salt, then taste and adjust the seasoning, adding more salt if necessary.

spiced black-eyed beans & mushrooms

ingredients

serves 4

1 onion, roughly chopped

4 large garlic cloves, roughly chopped

2.5-cm/1-inch piece fresh ginger, roughly chopped

4 tbsp sunflower or olive oil

1 tsp ground cumin

1 tsp ground coriander

$\frac{1}{2}$ tsp ground fennel

1 tsp ground turmeric

$\frac{1}{2}$–1 tsp chilli powder

175 g/6 oz canned chopped tomatoes

400 g/14 oz canned black-eyed beans, drained and rinsed

115 g/4 oz large flat mushrooms, wiped and cut into bite-sized pieces

$\frac{1}{2}$ tsp salt, or to taste

175 ml/6 fl oz warm water

1 tbsp chopped fresh mint

1 tbsp chopped fresh coriander leaves

Indian bread, to serve

method

1 Purée the onion, garlic and ginger in a food processor or blender.

2 Heat the oil in a medium saucepan over a medium heat and add the puréed ingredients. Cook for 4–5 minutes, then add the cumin, ground coriander, ground fennel, turmeric and chilli powder. Stir-fry for about a minute, then add the tomatoes. Cook until the tomatoes are pulpy and the juice has evaporated.

3 Add the black-eyed beans, mushrooms and salt. Stir well and pour in the warm water, bring to the boil, cover the pan and reduce the heat to low. Simmer for 8–10 minutes, stirring halfway through.

4 Stir in the chopped mint and coriander and remove from the heat. Transfer to a serving dish and serve with Indian bread.

lentils with fresh chillies, mint & coriander

ingredients

serves 4

85 g/3 oz red split lentils (masoor dhal)

85 g/3 oz skinless split chickpeas (channa dhal)

3 tbsp sunflower or olive oil

1 onion, finely chopped

2–3 fresh green chillies, chopped (deseeded if you like)

2 tsp garlic purée

2 tsp ginger purée

1 tsp ground cumin

600 ml/1 pint warm water

1 tsp salt, or to taste

1 tbsp chopped fresh mint

1 tbsp chopped fresh coriander leaves

55 g/2 oz unsalted butter

1 fresh green chilli and 1 small tomato, deseeded and cut into julienne strips, to garnish

method

1 Wash the lentils and chickpeas together until the water runs clear and leave to soak for 30 minutes.

2 Heat the oil in a medium saucepan, preferably non-stick, over a medium heat and add the onion, chillies and garlic and ginger purées. Stir-fry the mixture until it begins to brown.

3 Drain the lentils and chickpeas and add to the onion mixture together with the cumin. Reduce the heat to low and stir-fry for 2–3 minutes, then pour in the warm water. Bring to the boil, reduce the heat to low, cover and simmer for 25–30 minutes.

4 Stir in the salt, mint, fresh coriander and butter. Stir until the butter has melted, then remove from the heat. Serve garnished with the strips of chilli and tomato.

sweet-&-sour lentils

ingredients

serves 4

250 g/9 oz split yellow lentils
(chana dhal)
1.2 litres/2 pints water
2 bay leaves, torn
3 fresh chillies, sliced once,
but left whole
½ tsp ground turmeric
½ tsp asafoetida
3 tbsp vegetable or groundnut oil
½ onion, finely chopped
2-cm/¾-inch piece fresh ginger,
finely chopped
30 g/1 oz creamed coconut, grated
1 fresh green chilli, deseeded or
not, to taste, and chopped
1½ tbsp sugar
1½ tbsp tamarind paste or chutney
½ tsp garam masala
¼ tsp ground cumin
¼ tsp ground coriander
salt

to garnish

15 g/½ oz ghee, melted, or 1 tbsp
vegetable or groundnut oil
1 tsp garam masala
chopped fresh coriander

method

1 Put the lentils and water in a large saucepan with a lid
over a high heat and bring to the boil, skimming the
surface as necessary. When the foam stops rising, stir
in the bay leaves, chillies, turmeric and asafoetida.
Half-cover the pan and leave the lentils to continue
simmering for about 40 minutes, or until they are very
tender, but not reduced to a mush, and all the liquid
has been absorbed.

2 When the lentils are almost tender, heat the oil in a
kadhai, wok or large frying pan over a medium-high
heat. Add the onion and ginger and fry, stirring
frequently, for 5–8 minutes.

3 Stir in the coconut, green chilli, sugar, tamarind paste,
garam masala, cumin and ground coriander and stir
for about 1 minute.

4 When the lentils are tender, add them to the spice
mixture with the bay leaves, chillies and any liquid left
in the saucepan, and stir around to blend together.
Taste and add salt, if necessary, and extra sugar and
tamarind, if desired.

5 Transfer the lentils to a serving dish and drizzle the hot
ghee over the top. Sprinkle with garam masala and
coriander and serve immediately

mixed lentils with five-spice seasoning

ingredients

serves 4

125 g/4½ oz red split lentils (masoor dhal)

125 g/4½ oz skinless split mung beans (mung dhal)

900 ml/1½ pints hot water

1 tsp ground turmeric

1 tsp salt, or to taste

1 tbsp lemon juice

2 tbsp sunflower or olive oil

¼ tsp black mustard seeds

¼ tsp cumin seeds

¼ tsp nigella seeds

¼ tsp fennel seeds

4–5 fenugreek seeds

2–3 dried red chillies

1 small tomato, deseeded and cut into strips, and fresh coriander sprigs, to garnish

Indian bread, to serve

method

1 Mix the lentils and beans together and wash until the water runs clear. Put them into a saucepan with the hot water. Bring to the boil and reduce the heat slightly. Let it boil for 5–6 minutes, and when the foam subsides, add the turmeric, reduce the heat to low, cover and cook for 20 minutes. Add the salt and lemon juice and beat the dhal with a wire whisk. Add a little more hot water if the dhal is too thick.

2 Heat the oil in a small saucepan over a medium heat. When hot, but not smoking, add the mustard seeds. As soon as they begin to pop, reduce the heat to low and add the cumin seeds, nigella seeds, fennel seeds, fenugreek seeds and dried chillies. Let the spices sizzle until the seeds begin to pop and the chillies have blackened. Pour the contents of the saucepan over the lentils, scraping off every bit from the saucepan.

3 Turn off the heat and keep the saucepan covered until you are ready to serve. Transfer to a serving dish and garnish with tomato strips and coriander sprigs. Serve with Indian bread.

snacks & accompaniments

onion bhajis

ingredients

serves 4

150 g/5½ oz gram flour
1 tsp salt, or to taste
small pinch of bicarbonate
    of soda
25 g/1 oz ground rice
1 tsp fennel seeds
1 tsp cumin seeds
2 fresh green chillies, finely
    chopped (deseeded if
    you like)
2 large onions, about
    400 g/14 oz, sliced into
    half-rings and separated
15 g/½ oz fresh coriander,
    including the tender stalks,
    finely chopped
200 ml/7 fl oz water
sunflower or olive oil,
    for deep-frying
tomato or mango chutney,
    to serve

method

1 Sift the gram flour into a large bowl and add the salt, bicarbonate of soda, ground rice and fennel and cumin seeds. Mix together thoroughly, then add the chillies, onions and coriander. Gradually pour in the water and mix until a thick batter is formed and all the other ingredients are thoroughly coated with it.

2 Heat enough oil for deep-frying in a wok, deep saucepan or deep-fat fryer over a medium heat to 180°C/350°F, or until a cube of bread browns in 30 seconds. If the oil is not hot enough, the bhajis will be soggy. Add as many small amounts (about ½ tablespoon) of the batter as will fit in a single layer, without overcrowding. Reduce the heat slightly and cook the bhajis for 8–10 minutes, until golden brown and crisp.

3 Remove and drain on kitchen paper. Keep hot in a low oven while you cook the remaining batter.

4 Serve hot with chutney.

golden cauliflower pakoras

ingredients

serves 4

vegetable or groundnut oil,
   for deep-frying
400 g/14 oz cauliflower florets
chutney, to serve

batter

140 g/5 oz gram flour
2 tsp ground coriander
1 tsp garam masala
1 tsp salt
½ tsp ground turmeric
pinch of chilli powder
15 g/½ oz ghee, melted,
   or 1 tbsp vegetable or
   groundnut oil
1 tsp lemon juice
150 ml/5 fl oz cold water
2 tsp nigella seeds

method

1 To make the batter, stir the gram flour, coriander, garam masala, salt, turmeric and chilli powder into a large bowl. Make a well in the centre, add the ghee and lemon juice with 2 tablespoons of the water, and stir together to make a thick batter.

2 Slowly beat in enough of the remaining water with an electric hand-held mixer or a whisk to make a smooth batter about the same thickness as double cream. Stir in the nigella seeds. Cover the bowl and set aside to stand for at least 30 minutes.

3 When you are ready to fry, heat enough oil for deep-frying in a wok, deep-fat fryer or large heavy-based saucepan until it reaches 180°C/350°F, or until a cube of bread browns in 30 seconds. Dip one cauliflower floret at a time into the batter and let any excess batter fall back into the bowl, then drop it into the hot oil. Add a few more dipped florets, without overcrowding the pan, and fry for about 3 minutes, or until golden brown and crisp.

4 Use a slotted spoon to remove the fritters from the oil and drain well on crumpled kitchen paper. Continue frying until all the cauliflower florets and batter have been used. Serve the hot fritters with chutney for dipping.

vegetable samosas

ingredients

makes 12

3 tbsp sunflower or olive oil

½ tsp black mustard seeds

1 tsp cumin seeds

1 tsp fennel seeds

1 onion, finely chopped

2 fresh green chillies, finely
chopped (deseeded if you like)

2 tsp ginger purée

½ tsp ground turmeric

1 tsp ground coriander

1 tsp ground cumin

½ tsp chilli powder

350 g/12 oz boiled potatoes,
cut into bite-sized pieces

125 g/4½ oz frozen peas, thawed

1 tsp salt, or to taste

2 tbsp chopped fresh coriander
leaves

12 sheets filo pastry, about
28 x 18 cm/11 x 7 inches

55 g/2 oz butter, melted,
plus extra for greasing

chutney, to serve

method

1 Heat the oil in a saucepan over a medium heat and
add the mustard seeds, followed by the cumin and
fennel seeds. Add the onion, chillies and ginger purée
and cook, stirring frequently, for 5–6 minutes.

2 Add the ground spices and cook, stirring, for 1 minute.
Add the potatoes, peas and salt and stir until the
vegetables are thoroughly coated with the spices. Stir
in the coriander and remove from the heat. Leave to
cool completely.

3 Line a baking sheet with baking paper. Place a sheet
of filo pastry on a board and brush well with the
melted butter. Keep the remaining pastry sheets
covered with a moist cloth or clingfilm. Fold the
buttered pastry sheet in half lengthways, brush with
some more melted butter and fold lengthways again.

4 Place about 1 tablespoon of the vegetable filling on
the bottom right-hand corner of the pastry sheet and
fold over to form a triangle. Continue folding to the
top of the sheet, maintaining the shape. Transfer to the
prepared baking sheet and brush with melted butter.
Repeat with the rest of the filo pastry and filling.

5 Bake in a preheated oven, 180°C/350°F/Gas Mark 4, for
20 minutes, or until browned. Serve hot with chutney.

deep-fried potato balls

ingredients

serves 4

450 g/1 lb potatoes, boiled and
 diced
1 onion, chopped
2.5-cm/1-inch piece fresh ginger,
 finely chopped
1 fresh green chilli, deseeded and
 finely chopped
1 tbsp chopped fresh coriander
1 tbsp lemon juice
2 tsp aamchoor (dried mango
 powder)
vegetable oil, for deep-frying
salt
chutney, to serve

batter

115 g/4 oz gram flour
¼ tsp baking powder
¼ tsp chilli powder
about 150 ml/5 fl oz water
salt

method

1 To make the batter, sift the flour, baking powder, chilli
 powder and a pinch of salt into a bowl. Gradually, stir
 in enough cold water to make a smooth batter. Cover
 with clingfilm and reserve.

2 Place the potatoes, onion, ginger, chilli, coriander,
 lemon juice and amchoor in a separate bowl. Mix
 together well with a wooden spoon, breaking up
 the potatoes. Season with salt to taste. Break off small
 pieces of the mixture and form into balls between the
 palms of your hands.

3 Heat enough oil for deep-frying in a wok, deep-fat fryer
 or large heavy-based saucepan to 180°C/350°F, or until
 a cube of bread browns in 30 seconds. When the oil is
 hot, dip the potato balls in the batter, using a fork, and
 add to the oil, in batches. Deep-fry for 3–4 minutes,
 until golden brown. Remove with a slotted spoon and
 drain on kitchen paper. Keep each batch warm while
 you cook the remainder. Serve hot, with chutney.

spicy pancakes

ingredients

serves 6

140 g/5 oz basmati rice, soaked for 2–3 hours in cold water and drained

140 g/5 oz black lentils, soaked for 2–3 hours in cold water and drained

2 fresh green chillies, deseeded and finely chopped

1 tsp dark brown sugar

300 ml/10 fl oz water

1.25 kg/2 lb 12 oz potatoes

3 tbsp grated fresh coconut

2.5-cm/1-inch piece fresh ginger, finely chopped

4 tbsp ghee or vegetable oil, plus extra for frying

2 tsp black mustard seeds

2 tsp cumin seeds

1 tsp ground turmeric

3 tbsp chopped fresh coriander

salt

fresh mint sprigs, to garnish

chutney, to serve

method

1 Place the rice and black lentils in a food processor and process until ground. Tip into a bowl. Stir in half the chillies, the sugar and a pinch of salt. Gradually add the water and mix to a smooth batter. Cover and leave to stand in a warm place overnight.

2 Cook the potatoes in lightly salted boiling water for 20–25 minutes, or until tender. Drain and mash. Mix the remaining chillies, coconut and ginger to a paste.

3 Heat the ghee in a large, heavy-based frying pan, add the mustard and cumin seeds and stir until they give off their aroma. Stir in the coconut and ginger paste and cook for 1 minute, then add the mashed potatoes, turmeric and coriander and cook, stirring, for 5 minutes. Remove from the heat.

4 Heat a little ghee in a 20-cm/8-inch frying pan. Stir the batter. Pour one-sixth into the frying pan, tilting the pan to spread it over the base. Cook for 1–2 minutes, or until the underside is golden. Flip over and cook the other side for 2 minutes. Transfer to a plate and keep warm while you cook the remaining pancakes, adding more ghee as required. Divide the filling between the pancakes and fold in half. Return them to the frying pan, in batches, and fry for 30 seconds on each side. Garnish with fresh mint sprigs and serve with chutney.

plantain chips

ingredients

serves 4

4 ripe plantains
1 tsp mild, medium or hot curry
powder, to taste
vegetable or groundnut oil,
for deep-frying
mango chutney, to serve

method

1 Peel the plantains, then cut crossways into 3-mm/
⅛-inch slices. Put the slices in a bowl, sprinkle over
the curry powder and use your hands to toss lightly
together.

2 Heat enough oil for deep-frying in a wok, deep-fat
fryer or large heavy-based saucepan to 180°C/350°F,
or until a cube of bread browns in 30 seconds. Add
as many plantain slices as will fit in the pan without
overcrowding and fry for 2 minutes, or until golden.

3 Remove the plantain chips from the pan with a slotted
spoon and drain well on crumpled kitchen paper.
Serve hot with mango chutney.

spiced basmati rice

ingredients

serves 4–6

225 g/8 oz basmati rice
30 g/1 oz ghee or 2 tbsp vegetable
    or groundnut oil
5 green cardamom pods, bruised
5 cloves
½ cinnamon stick
1 tsp fennel seeds
½ tsp black mustard seeds
2 bay leaves
450 ml/16 fl oz water
1½ tsp salt, or to taste
pepper

method

1 Rinse the basmati rice in several changes of water until the water runs clear, then leave to soak for 30 minutes. Drain and set aside until ready to cook.

2 Melt the ghee in a flameproof casserole or large saucepan with a tight-fitting lid over a medium–high heat. Add the spices and bay leaves and stir for 30 seconds. Stir the rice into the casserole so the grains are coated with ghee. Stir in the water and salt and bring to the boil.

3 Reduce the heat to as low as possible and cover the casserole tightly. Simmer, without lifting the lid, for 8–10 minutes, until the grains are tender and all the liquid is absorbed.

4 Turn off the heat and use 2 forks to fluff up the rice. Adjust the seasoning, adding salt and pepper if necessary. Re-cover the pan and leave to stand for 5 minutes.

mint & coriander rice with toasted pine kernels

ingredients

serves 4

good pinch of saffron threads, pounded

2 tbsp hot milk

225 g/8 oz basmati rice

2 tbsp sunflower or olive oil

5-cm/2-inch piece cinnamon stick, broken in half

4 green cardamom pods, bruised

2 star anise

2 bay leaves

450 ml/16 fl oz lukewarm water

3 tbsp fresh coriander leaves, finely chopped

2 tbsp fresh mint leaves, finely chopped, or 1 tsp dried mint

1 tsp salt, or to taste

25 g/1 oz pine kernels

method

1 Soak the pounded saffron threads in the hot milk and set aside until you are ready to use. Wash the rice in several changes of cold water until the water runs clear. Leave to soak in fresh cold water for 20 minutes, then leave to drain in a colander.

2 Heat the oil in a medium heavy-based saucepan over a low heat. Add the cinnamon, cardamom, star anise and bay leaves and leave to sizzle gently for 20–25 seconds. Add the rice and stir well to ensure that the grains are coated with the flavoured oil.

3 Add the water, stir once and bring to the boil. Add the saffron and milk, coriander, mint and salt and boil for 2–3 minutes. Cover tightly, reduce the heat to very low and cook for 7–8 minutes. Turn off the heat and leave to stand, covered, for 7–8 minutes.

4 Meanwhile, preheat a small heavy-based frying pan over a medium heat, add the pine kernels and cook, stirring, until lightly toasted. Transfer to a plate and leave to cool.

5 Add half the toasted pine kernels to the rice and fluff up the rice with a fork. Transfer to a serving dish, garnish with the remaining pine kernels and serve immediately.

lemon-laced basmati rice

ingredients

serves 4

225 g/8 oz basmati rice

2 tbsp sunflower or olive oil

½ tsp black or brown mustard seeds

10–12 curry leaves, preferably fresh

25 g/1 oz cashew nuts

¼ tsp ground turmeric

1 tsp salt, or to taste

450 ml/16 fl oz hot water

2 tbsp lemon juice

1 tbsp snipped fresh chives, to garnish

method

1 Wash the rice in several changes of cold water until the water runs clear. Leave to soak in fresh cold water for 20 minutes, then leave to drain in a colander.

2 Heat the oil in a non-stick saucepan over a medium heat. When hot, but not smoking, add the mustard seeds, followed by the curry leaves and the cashew nuts (in that order).

3 Stir in the turmeric, quickly followed by the rice and salt. Cook, stirring, for 1 minute, then add the hot water and lemon juice. Stir once, bring to the boil and boil for 2 minutes. Cover tightly, reduce the heat to very low and cook for 8 minutes. Turn off the heat and leave to stand, covered, for 6–7 minutes.

4 Fork through the rice and transfer to a serving dish. Garnish with the chives and serve immediately.

coconut rice

ingredients

serves 4–6

225 g/8 oz basmati rice
450 ml/16 fl oz water
60 g/2¼ oz creamed coconut
2 tbsp mustard oil
1½ tsp salt

method

1 Rinse the basmati rice in several changes of water until the water runs clear, then leave to soak for 30 minutes. Drain and set aside until ready to cook.

2 Bring the water to the boil in a small saucepan, stir in the creamed coconut until it dissolves and then set aside.

3 Heat the mustard oil in a large frying pan or saucepan with a lid over a high heat until it smokes. Turn off the heat and leave the mustard oil to cool completely.

4 When you are ready to cook, reheat the mustard oil over a medium–high heat. Add the rice and stir until all the grains are coated in oil. Add the water with the dissolved coconut and bring to the boil.

5 Reduce the heat to its lowest setting, stir in the salt and cover the pan tightly. Simmer, without lifting the lid, for 8–10 minutes, until the grains are tender and all the liquid is absorbed.

6 Turn off the heat and use 2 forks to mix the rice. Adjust the seasoning, if necessary. Re-cover the pan and leave the rice to stand for 5 minutes.

spiced basmati pilau

ingredients

serves 4

500 g/1 lb 2 oz basmati rice
175 g/6 oz broccoli, trimmed
6 tbsp vegetable oil
2 large onions, chopped
225 g/8 oz mushrooms, sliced
2 garlic cloves, crushed
6 green cardamom pods, bruised
6 whole cloves
8 black peppercorns
1 cinnamon stick or piece of
    cassia bark
1 tsp ground turmeric
1.2 litres/2 pints vegetable stock
    or water
55 g/2 oz seedless raisins
55 g/2 oz unsalted pistachios,
    roughly chopped
salt and pepper

method

1 Place the rice in a sieve and wash well under cold
   running water. Drain. Trim off most of the broccoli stalk
   and cut the head into small florets, then quarter the stalk
   lengthways and cut diagonally into 1-cm/½-inch pieces.

2 Heat the oil in a large saucepan. Add the onions and
   broccoli stalks and cook over a low heat, stirring
   frequently, for 3 minutes. Add the mushrooms, rice,
   garlic and spices and cook for 1 minute, stirring, until
   the rice is coated in oil.

3 Add the stock and season to taste with salt and pepper.
   Stir in the broccoli florets and return the mixture to the
   boil. Cover, reduce the heat and cook over a low heat
   for 15 minutes without uncovering the pan.

4 Remove the pan from the heat and leave the pilau to
   stand for 5 minutes without uncovering. Remove the
   whole spices, add the raisins and pistachios and gently
   fork through to fluff up the grains. Serve the pilau hot.

chapatis

ingredients

makes 16

400 g/14 oz chapati flour (atta),
    plus extra for dusting
1 tsp salt
½ tsp granulated sugar
2 tbsp sunflower or olive oil
250 ml/9 fl oz lukewarm water

method

1 Mix the chapati flour, salt and sugar together in a large bowl. Add the oil and work well into the flour mixture with your fingertips. Gradually add the water, mixing at the same time. When the dough is formed, transfer to a work surface and knead for 4–5 minutes. The dough is ready when all the excess moisture is absorbed by the flour. Alternatively, mix the dough in a food processor. Wrap the dough in clingfilm and leave to rest for 30 minutes.

2 Divide the dough in half, then cut each half into 8 equal-sized pieces. Form each piece into a ball and flatten into a round cake. Dust each cake lightly in the flour and roll out to a 15-cm/6-inch round. Keep the remaining cakes covered while you are working on one. The chapatis will cook better when freshly rolled out, so roll out and cook one at a time.

3 Preheat a heavy-based cast-iron griddle (tawa) or a large heavy-based frying pan over a medium–high heat. Put a chapati on the griddle and cook for 30 seconds. Turn over and cook until bubbles begin to appear on the surface. Turn over again. Press the edges down gently with a clean cloth to encourage the chapati to puff up. Cook until brown patches appear on the underside. Remove from the pan and keep hot by wrapping in a piece of foil lined with kitchen paper. Repeat with the remaining dough cakes.

chilli-coriander naan

ingredients

makes 8

450 g/1 lb plain flour
2 tsp sugar
1 tsp salt
1 tsp baking powder
1 egg
250 ml/9 fl oz milk
2 tbsp sunflower or olive oil,
   plus extra for oiling
2 fresh red chillies, chopped
   (deseeded if you like)
15 g/½ oz fresh coriander leaves,
   chopped
2 tbsp butter, melted

method

1 Sift the flour, sugar, salt and baking powder together into a large bowl. Whisk the egg and milk together, then gradually add to the flour and mix until a dough is formed.

2 Transfer the dough to a work surface, make a depression in the centre of the dough and add the oil. Knead for 3–4 minutes, until you have a smooth and pliable dough. Wrap the dough in clingfilm and leave to rest for 1 hour.

3 Divide the dough into 8 equal-sized pieces, form each piece into a ball and flatten into a thick cake. Cover with clingfilm and leave to rest for 10–15 minutes.

4 Preheat the grill to high, line a grill pan with a piece of foil and brush with oil. Roll each flattened cake into a 12.5-cm/5-inch round and pull the lower end gently. Carefully roll out again, maintaining the teardrop shape, to about 23 cm/9 inches in diameter.

5 Mix the chillies and coriander together, then spread on the surface of the naans. Press gently so that the mixture sticks to the dough. Transfer a naan to the prepared grill pan and cook until slightly puffed and brown. Turn over and cook the other side, until lightly browned. Remove from the grill and brush with the melted butter. Wrap in a tea towel while you cook the remaining naans.

pooris

ingredients

makes 12

225 g/8 oz wholemeal flour, sifted,
    plus extra for dusting
½ teaspoon salt
30 g/1 oz ghee, melted
100–150 ml/3½–5 fl oz water
vegetable or groundnut oil,
    for deep-frying

method

1 Put the flour and salt into a bowl and drizzle the ghee over the surface. Gradually stir in the water until a stiff dough forms. Turn out the dough onto a lightly floured surface and knead for 10 minutes, or until it is smooth and elastic. Shape the dough into a ball and place it in a clean bowl, then cover with a damp tea towel and leave to rest for 20 minutes.

2 Divide the dough into 12 equal-sized pieces and roll each into a ball. Flatten each ball of dough between your palms, then thinly roll it out on a lightly floured work surface into a 13-cm/5-inch round. Continue until all the dough balls are rolled out.

3 Heat at least 7.5 cm/3 inches oil in a wok, deep-fat fryer or large frying pan until it reaches 180°C/350°F, or until a cube of bread browns in 30 seconds. Drop one poori into the hot fat and fry for about 10 seconds, or until it puffs up. Use 2 large spoons to flip the poori over and spoon some hot oil over the top.

4 Use the 2 spoons to lift the poori from the oil and let any excess oil drip back into the pan. Drain the poori on crumpled kitchen paper and serve immediately. Continue until all the pooris are fried, making sure the oil returns to the correct temperature before you add another poori.

cucumber raita

ingredients

serves 4–5

1 small cucumber
175 g/6 oz whole milk natural
    yogurt
¼ tsp granulated sugar
¼ tsp salt
1 tsp cumin seeds
10–12 black peppercorns
¼ tsp paprika

method

1 Peel the cucumber and scoop out the seeds.
   Cut the flesh into bite-sized pieces and set aside.

2 Put the yogurt in a bowl and beat with a fork until
   smooth. Add the sugar and salt and mix well.

3 Preheat a small heavy-based saucepan over a
   medium–high heat. When the pan is hot, turn off the
   heat and add the cumin seeds and peppercorns. Stir
   around for 40–50 seconds, until they release their
   aroma. Remove from the pan and leave to cool for
   5 minutes, then crush in a mortar with a pestle or on
   a hard surface with a rolling pin.

4 Reserve ¼ teaspoon of this mixture and stir the
   remainder into the yogurt. Add the cucumber and stir
   to mix. Transfer the raita to a serving dish and sprinkle
   with the reserved toasted spices and the paprika.

mint & spinach chutney

ingredients

serves 4–6

55 g/2 oz tender fresh spinach
  leaves
3 tbsp fresh mint leaves
2 tbsp chopped fresh coriander
  leaves
1 small red onion, roughly
  chopped
1 small garlic clove, chopped
1 fresh green chilli, chopped
  (deseeded if you like)
2½ tsp granulated sugar
1 tbsp tamarind juice or juice
  of ½ lemon

method

1 Put all the ingredients in a blender or food processor
  and blend until smooth, adding a little water to enable
  the blades to move, if necessary.

2 Transfer to a serving bowl, cover and chill in the
  refrigerator for at least 30 minutes before serving.

tomato kachumbar

ingredients

serves 6

125 ml/4 fl oz lime juice
½ tsp sugar
6 tomatoes, chopped
½ cucumber, chopped
8 spring onions, chopped
1 fresh green chilli, deseeded
    and chopped
1 tbsp chopped fresh coriander
1 tbsp chopped fresh mint
salt

method

1 Mix the lime juice, sugar and a pinch of salt together in a large bowl and stir until the sugar has completely dissolved.

2 Add the tomatoes, cucumber, spring onions, chilli, coriander and mint and toss well to mix.

3 Cover with clingfilm and leave the mixture to chill in the refrigerator for at least 30 minutes. Toss the vegetables before serving.

coriander chutney

ingredients

makes 225 g/8 oz

1½ tbsp lemon juice

1½ tbsp water

85 g/3 oz fresh coriander leaves
and stems, roughly chopped

2 tbsp chopped fresh coconut

1 small shallot, very finely chopped

5-mm/¼-inch piece fresh ginger,
chopped

1 fresh green chilli, deseeded
and chopped

½ tsp sugar

½ tsp salt

pinch of pepper

method

1 Put the lemon juice and water in a small food
processor, add half the coriander and whizz until
it is blended and a slushy paste forms. Gradually
add the remaining coriander and whizz until it is all
blended, scraping down the sides of the processor,
if necessary. If you don't have a processor that will
cope with this small amount, use a pestle and mortar,
adding the coriander in small amounts.

2 Add the remaining ingredients and continue whizzing
until they are all finely chopped and blended. Taste and
adjust any of the seasonings, if you like. Transfer to a
non-metallic bowl, cover and chill for up to 3 days
before serving.

mango chutney

ingredients

makes 250 g/9 oz

1 large mango, about 400 g/14 oz, peeled, stoned and finely chopped

2 tbsp lime juice

1 tbsp vegetable or groundnut oil

2 shallots, finely chopped

1 garlic clove, finely chopped

2 fresh green chillies, deseeded and finely sliced

1 tsp black mustard seeds

1 tsp coriander seeds

5 tbsp palm sugar or soft light brown sugar

5 tbsp white wine vinegar

1 tsp salt

pinch of ground ginger

method

1 Put the mango in a non-metallic bowl with the lime juice and set aside.

2 Heat the oil in a large frying pan or saucepan over a medium–high heat. Add the shallots and cook for 3 minutes. Add the garlic and chillies and stir for a further 2 minutes, or until the shallots are soft but not brown. Add the mustard seeds and coriander seeds and then stir around.

3 Add the mango to the pan with the palm sugar, vinegar, salt and ground ginger and stir around. Reduce the heat to its lowest setting and simmer for 10 minutes, until the liquid thickens and the mango becomes sticky.

4 Remove from the heat and leave to cool completely. Transfer to an airtight container, cover and chill for 3 days before using.

lime pickle

ingredients

makes 225 g/8 oz

12 limes, halved and deseeded
115 g/4 oz salt
70 g/2½ oz chilli powder
25 g/1 oz mustard powder
25 g/1 oz ground fenugreek
1 tbsp ground turmeric
300 ml/10 fl oz mustard oil
15 g/½ oz yellow mustard seeds,
    crushed
½ tsp asafoetida

method

1 Cut each lime half into 4 pieces and pack them into a large sterilized jar, sprinkling over the salt at the same time. Cover and leave to stand in a warm place for 10–14 days, or until the limes have turned brown and softened.

2 Mix the chilli powder, mustard powder, fenugreek and turmeric together in a small bowl and add to the jar of limes. Stir to mix, then re-cover and leave to stand for 2 days.

3 Transfer the lime mixture to a heatproof bowl. Heat the mustard oil in a heavy-based frying pan. Add the mustard seeds and asafoetida to the pan and cook, stirring constantly, until the oil is very hot and just beginning to smoke.

4 Pour the oil and spices over the limes and mix well. Cover and leave to cool. When cool, pack into a sterilized jar, seal and store in a sunny place for 1 week before serving.

desserts

indian rice dessert

ingredients

serves 4

good pinch of saffron threads,
  pounded
2 tbsp hot milk
40 g/1½ oz ghee or unsalted butter
55 g/2 oz ground rice
25 g/1 oz flaked almonds
25 g/1 oz seedless raisins
600 ml/1 pint full-fat milk
450 ml/16 fl oz evaporated milk
55 g/2 oz caster sugar
12 ready-to-eat dried apricots,
  sliced
1 tsp freshly ground cardamom
  seeds
½ tsp freshly grated nutmeg
2 tbsp rosewater

to decorate

25 g/1 oz walnut pieces
15 g/½ oz shelled unsalted
  pistachio nuts

method

1 Place the pounded saffron in the hot milk and leave
   to soak until needed. Reserve 2 teaspoons of the ghee
   and melt the remainder in a heavy-based saucepan
   over a low heat. Add the ground rice, almonds and
   raisins and cook, stirring, for 2 minutes. Add the full-fat
   milk, increase the heat to medium and cook, stirring,
   until it begins to bubble gently. Reduce the heat to
   low and cook, stirring frequently, for 10–12 minutes,
   to prevent the mixture from sticking to the pan.

2 Add the evaporated milk, sugar and apricots, reserving
   a few slices to decorate. Cook, stirring, until the mixture
   thickens to the consistency of a pouring custard.

3 Add the reserved saffron and milk mixture, the
   cardamom, nutmeg and rosewater, stir to distribute
   well and remove from the heat. Leave to cool, then
   cover and chill in the refrigerator for at least 2 hours.

4 Melt the reserved ghee in a small saucepan over a low
   heat. Add the walnuts and cook, stirring, until they
   brown a little. Remove and drain on kitchen paper.
   Brown the pistachio nuts in the saucepan, remove and
   drain on kitchen paper. Leave the pistachio nuts to
   cool, then lightly crush.

5 Serve the dessert decorated with the fried nuts and
   the reserved apricot slices.

sago & coconut pudding

ingredients

serves 4

½ fresh coconut
225 ml/8 fl oz water
850 ml/1½ pints milk
85 g/3 oz caster sugar
25 g/1 oz raisins
55 g/2 oz sago
seeds from 6–8 green
    cardamom pods
25 g/1 oz flaked almonds,
    for sprinkling

method

1 To prepare the coconut milk, remove the flesh from the coconut half-shell and grate it. Place in a food processor or blender, add the water and process until smooth. Strain through a sieve into a jug, pressing down on the coconut with the back of a wooden spoon. Discard the contents of the sieve and reserve the coconut milk.

2 Bring the 850 ml/1½ pints milk to the boil in a large heavy-based saucepan and continue to boil until it has reduced to 600 ml/1 pint. Reduce the heat, add the sugar and stir until dissolved. Stir in the raisins and sago. Simmer gently for 6–8 minutes, or until the sago is cooked.

3 Remove the saucepan from the heat and stir in the coconut milk and cardamom seeds, then pour into individual serving dishes. Sprinkle with the almonds and leave to cool before serving.

mango kulfi

ingredients

serves 6–8

375 g/13 oz canned evaporated milk

300 ml/10 fl oz single cream

25 g/1 oz ground almonds

115–140 g/4–5 oz granulated sugar

450 g/1 lb mango purée

1 tsp freshly ground cardamom seeds

25 g/1 oz shelled unsalted pistachio nuts, to decorate

method

1 Pour the evaporated milk and cream into a heavy-based saucepan and stir to mix. Put over a medium heat. Mix the ground almonds and sugar together, then add to the milk mixture. Cook, stirring, for 6–8 minutes, until the mixture thickens slightly.

2 Remove from the heat and leave the mixture to cool completely, stirring from time to time to prevent a skin forming. When completely cold, stir in the mango purée and ground cardamom.

3 Meanwhile, preheat a small saucepan over a medium heat, add the pistachio nuts and toast for 2–3 minutes. Leave to cool, then lightly crush. Store in an airtight container until required.

4 Kulfi is set in traditional conical-shaped plastic or steel moulds, which you can buy from Asian stores, but you can use decorative individual jelly moulds or ice lolly moulds instead. Fill the containers of your choice with the kulfi mixture and freeze for 5–6 hours. Transfer the kulfi to the refrigerator for 40 minutes, then invert onto serving dishes. Serve sprinkled with the crushed pistachio nuts to decorate.

saffron & almond kulfi

ingredients
makes 4

½ tsp saffron threads, 'toasted'
in a deep frying pan over
a high heat
75 ml/2½ fl oz milk
1 tbsp ground rice
½ tbsp ground almonds
225 ml/8 fl oz canned
evaporated milk
225 ml/8 fl oz double cream
2 tbsp caster sugar
2 tbsp chopped toasted blanched
almonds, to serve

method

1 Put the milk in the frying pan over a medium–high heat, add the toasted saffron threads and heat just until small bubbles appear around the edge. Remove the pan from the heat and leave the saffron to infuse for at least 15 minutes. Meanwhile, combine the ground rice and ground almonds in a heatproof bowl. Put a shallow freezerproof container into the freezer.

2 Reheat the milk and saffron just until small bubbles appear, then slowly beat the milk into the almond mixture, until smooth. Pour the evaporated milk into a pan and bring to the boil, stirring. Remove the pan and stir into the milk mixture. Stir in the cream and sugar.

3 Return the pan to a medium heat and simmer, stirring constantly, for 5–10 minutes until the mixture thickens, but do not boil. Set aside to cool, stirring frequently. Pour the saffron mixture into the freezerproof container and freeze for 30 minutes, then beat to break up any ice crystals. Beat every 30 minutes until the ice cream is thick and almost firm.

4 Divide the mixture equally between 4 kulfi moulds or ramekins. Cover and freeze until solid. To serve, dip a cloth in hot water, wring it out and rub it around the sides of the moulds or ramekins, then invert onto plates. Sprinkle with toasted almonds and serve.

almond & pistachio dessert

ingredients

serves 2

75 g/2¾ oz unsalted butter
200 g/7 oz ground almonds
200 g/7 oz sugar
150 ml/5 fl oz single cream
8 almonds, chopped
10 pistachio nuts, chopped

method

1 Melt the butter in a heavy-based saucepan, preferably non-stick, stirring well. Add the ground almonds, sugar and cream, stirring well. Reduce the heat and stir constantly for 10–12 minutes, scraping the base of the saucepan.

2 Increase the heat until the mixture turns a little darker in colour.

3 Transfer the almond mixture to a large, shallow serving dish and smooth the top with the back of a spoon.

4 Decorate the top of the dessert with the chopped almonds and pistachio nuts. Leave to set for 1 hour, then cut into diamond shapes and serve cold.

carrot halva

ingredients

serves 4–6

55 g/2 oz ghee or unsalted butter
2.5-cm/1-inch piece cinnamon
　　stick, halved
25 g/1 oz flaked almonds
25 g/1 oz cashew nuts
25 g /1 oz seedless raisins
450 g/1 lb grated carrots
600 ml/1 pint full-fat milk
125 g/4½ oz caster sugar
½ tsp freshly ground
　　cardamom seeds
½ tsp freshly grated nutmeg
50 ml/2 fl oz double cream
2 tbsp rosewater
vanilla ice cream or whipped
　　double cream, to serve

method

1 Melt the ghee in a heavy-based saucepan over a low
heat. Add the cinnamon stick and leave to sizzle gently
for 25–30 seconds. Add the almonds and cashew nuts
and cook, stirring, until lightly browned. Remove about
a dessertspoon of the nuts and reserve.

2 Add the raisins, carrots, milk and sugar to the saucepan,
increase the heat to medium and bring the milk to
boiling point. Continue to cook over a low–medium
heat for 15–20 minutes, until the milk evaporates
completely, stirring frequently, and scraping and
blending in any thickened milk that sticks to the side
of the saucepan. Don't allow any milk that is stuck to
the side to brown or burn, as this will give the dessert
an unpleasant flavour.

3 Stir in the cardamom, nutmeg, cream and rosewater.
Remove from the heat and leave to cool slightly, then
serve topped with a scoop of vanilla ice cream or
whipped double cream. Sprinkle over the reserved
nuts to decorate.

shrikhand with pomegranate

ingredients

serves 4

1 litre/1¾ pints natural yogurt
¼ tsp saffron threads
2 tbsp milk
55 g/2 oz caster sugar, or to taste
seeds from 2 green cardamom
    pods
2 pomegranates, or other
    exotic fruit

method

1 Line a sieve set over a bowl with a piece of muslin large
   enough to hang over the edge. Add the yogurt, then
   tie the corners of the muslin into a tight knot and tie
   them to a tap. Leave the bundle to hang over the sink
   for 4 hours, or until all the excess moisture drips away.

2 Put the saffron threads in a dry saucepan over a high
   heat and 'toast', stirring frequently, until you can smell
   the aroma. Immediately tip them out of the pan. Put
   the milk in the pan, return the saffron threads and
   warm just until bubbles appear around the edge,
   then set aside and leave to infuse.

3 When the yogurt is thick and creamy, put it in a bowl
   and stir in the sugar, cardamom seeds and saffron
   mixture and beat until smooth. Taste and add extra
   sugar, if desired. Cover and chill for at least 1 hour,
   until well chilled.

4 Meanwhile, to prepare the pomegranate seeds, cut the
   fruit in half and use a small teaspoon or your fingers to
   scoop out the seeds.

5 To serve, spoon the yogurt into individual bowls or
   plates and add the pomegranate seeds.

ginger ice cream with date & tamarind sauce

ingredients

serves 4–5

ice cream

1-litre/1¾-pint carton vanilla
   ice cream
2 tsp ground ginger
200 g/7 oz chopped crystallized
   ginger, to serve

tamarind sauce

55 g/2 oz seedless raisins
85 g/3 oz stoned dried dates
250 ml/9 fl oz boiling water
2 rounded tsp tamarind
   concentrate or 3 tbsp
   tamarind juice
25 g/1 oz molasses sugar

method

1 Leave the ice cream at room temperature for 35–40
   minutes to soften, then transfer to a bowl. Add the
   ground ginger and beat well. Return to the carton
   and freeze for 3–4 hours.

2 Meanwhile, to make the sauce, put the raisins and
   dates in a heatproof bowl, pour over the boiling water
   and leave to soak for 15–20 minutes. Transfer to a
   blender or food processor, add the tamarind and sugar
   and blend to a smooth purée. Transfer to a non-metallic
   bowl and leave to cool.

3 Put scoops of the ice cream into serving dishes and
   drizzle over the sauce. Arrange about 1 dessertspoon
   of crystallized ginger on top of each dessert and serve
   immediately. Serve any extra sauce separately.

sweet saffron rice with caramelized pineapple

ingredients

serves 4–6

good pinch of saffron threads, pounded and soaked in 2 tbsp hot milk

175 g/6 oz basmati rice, washed

½ fresh pineapple (225 g/8 oz prepared weight) peeled, with 'eyes' removed, and cut into bite-sized pieces

55 g/2 oz ghee or unsalted butter

150–175 g/5½–6 oz caster sugar

4 green cardamom pods, bruised

4 cloves

2 x 1-cm/½-inch pieces cinnamon stick

300 ml/10 fl oz warm water

melted butter or vegetable oil, for brushing

55 g/2 oz seedless raisins

25 g/1 oz toasted flaked almonds, to decorate

single cream, to serve

method

1 Melt 1 tablespoon of the ghee in a heavy-based frying pan over a low heat. Add the pineapple, sprinkle with 2 tablespoons of the sugar and increase the heat to high. Caramelize the pineapple, then remove from the heat.

2 Melt the remaining ghee. Add the cardamom pods, cloves and cinnamon stick and cook briefly, stirring. Add the rice, increase the heat slightly and cook, stirring, for 2–3 minutes. Add the saffron, milk and the warm water, boil for 2 minutes, then reduce the heat to low for 2–3 minutes. Remove from the heat.

3 Add one-third of the rice to a lidded ovenproof dish. Top with one-third of the raisins, followed by one third of the pineapple pieces and one-third of the remaining sugar. Repeat twice more, finishing with a layer of raisins, pineapple and sugar.

4 Soak a piece of greaseproof paper, crumple it, then place loosely over the top layer. Cover with foil and seal the edges. Put the lid on and bake in the centre of a preheated oven, 160°C/325°F/Gas Mark 3, for 35–40 minutes. Turn off the oven and leave the rice to stand in the oven for 10–15 minutes. Decorate with flaked almonds and serve with cream.

mango lassi

ingredients

serves 4–6

1 large mango, about 300 g/
    10½ oz, peeled, stoned and
    roughly chopped
700 ml/1¼ pints natural yogurt
250 ml/9 fl oz cold water
about 2 tbsp caster sugar,
    or to taste
fresh lime juice, to taste
ice cubes
ground ginger, to decorate
    (optional)

method

1 Put the mango flesh in a food processor or blender with the yogurt and whizz until smooth. Add the water and whizz again to blend.

2 The amount of sugar you will add depends on how sweet the mango is. Taste and stir in sugar to taste, then stir in the lime juice.

3 Fill 4 or 6 glasses with ice cubes and pour over the mango mixture. Lightly dust the top of each glass with ground ginger, if you like.

index